PRAISE FOR *THE NEXT ONE UP MINDSET*

"My entire career has been about getting prepared for the unknown and doing what I need to do in the moment to stay laser focused. The Next One Up Mindset approach beautifully outlines strategies that help condition the mind and body for the unexpected. Using these very same techniques, Grant helped me prepare for the 2018 Winter Olympic Games."

— AJA EVANS

Two-Time Olympian and 2014 Bronze Medalist, Women's Bobsled

"Grant hits the nail on the head in this book. He draws from the experiences of the best athletes in the world and shows you why they perform when the pressure is the highest. This is a must read for sports fans interested in the psychology of top-level athletes."

— RYAN MURPHY

Three-Time Olympic Gold Medalist and World Record Holder

"Not only does Grant Parr have an incredible podcast, 90% Mental, *he has now written an incredible book,* The Next One Up Mindset: How to Prepare for the Unknown. *Parr's book provides strategies to connect the mind and body to help anyone succeed when their number is called. Grant is a genuine man with a passion for helping people from all walks of life perform their best when it counts most."*

— BOB TEWKSBURY

Former MLB Player and Mental Performance Coach, Chicago Cubs

D0018874

"In The Next One Up Mindset, *Grant does a masterful job of weaving together compelling sports stories with concrete tools to increase performance in the competition that most of us call the 'world of work.' I found myself alternating between immersion in the stories and being intellectually challenged by the tools and concepts and how they apply to me and to the teams I lead. I recommend this book to anyone who wants to improve their performance in any way—whether on the field of play or on the field of life."*

— LORI LANGHOLZ

Chief Business Development Officer, BDO USA, LLP

"After reading The Next One Up Mindset, *I immediately grabbed a key concept and applied it to my coaching methods. Using inspirational examples combined with concrete techniques and concepts,* The Next One Up Mindset *will give athletes and coaches of all levels key takeaways that will help them be ready for their 'next one up' moment."*

— MIKE PEDERSON

Coach, Canadian National Women's Foil Team
Coach, 2008 Olympic USA Women's Foil Team

"Whether you're a seasoned athlete or someone looking to understand how mental strategies can help in your everyday life, Grant gives his clear insights into an often overlooked area in high performance. This book provides a unique toolkit for making sense of the winding path toward success and for better navigating your journey."

— TIFFANY ROBERTS SAHAYDAK

Olympic Gold Medalist
Head Coach, University of Central Florida Women's Soccer

"There's a big difference between practicing for your big moment and living that moment. Anyone who's stood at a start line or reached for the ball knows what I'm talking about. What happens in that split second of time can help you manifest your dreams. Thankfully, Grant Parr is here to help us create a plan, practice for that second, and point us to what really counts in that key moment to help you get off the block, catch the ball, or take that moment and make it yours."

— JOANNA BLOOR

CEO and Founder, The Amplify Lab
TED Talks Speaker

"Grant Parr gives you the foundations to influence yourself to step up to the plate and swing for the fences. He teaches you to be flexible in your journey to achieve sustained success."

— GREG ROMERO

Three-Time BMX Olympic Coach

"As a mental skills coach, Grant empowered our athletes through breath, visualization, and the tools to formulate positive self-talk. His book, The Next One Up Mindset: How to Prepare for the Unknown, *provides a mental skills blueprint for optimal performance from the inside out—mind to body and body to peak performance. It's a great read to maximize potential or for performance restoration."*

— SUE PHILLIPS

Head Coach, Archbishop Mitty High School Women's Basketball

"Grant Parr has found grace, humor, and wisdom in situations that would have soured others into bitterness. What's more, he's channeled this levity and knowledge into a podcast and now a book. The Next One Up Mindset *outlines how each of us can face unexpected opportunities with carefully developed skills. Greeting our next challenge, planned or unplanned, with a calm, grounded, and focused awareness; narrowing in on muscle memory and playfulness; finding our own foundation—this is how leaders and athletes, or really people in any endeavor, can ride at the bleeding edge of their capabilities.*

Reading his book, I was reminded of the exhilaration, fear, and transcendence I myself have felt when pushing my edge in rock climbing or mountaineering. Returning to the stressors of city life, they all looked diminished, manageable, so much easier by comparison."

— RAMAN FREY

Author, Mount Commerce: Beginnings of Incentive System Design
Founder, GP Dinners
Partner, AH Global

"Sports are as much of a mental game as they are a physical game. The mind is the most important part of our bodies that we have to work out as athletes. Muscles only grow after they have been worked through consistency, exhaustion, and proper coaching; the brain is no different. Confidence takes consistent practice to build up, and the most confident of players were forged through rejection, fatigue, failure, and doubt. Grant Parr is that coach for the mind! With his help, an athlete's mind will grow similarly to the way muscles grow as he is the coach pushing us through the exhaustion, redirecting the way we think about failure, and keeping athletes consistent! With his help, confidence is inevitable, and once you have the right mindset, 70 percent of the work is done!"

— A.J. ANDREWS

Professional Softball Player, Akron Racers
First Woman Awarded the Rawlings Gold Glove Award

"Grant Parr is one of the highest quality human beings I have been around in my athletic career. Early on in my high school football season, I was struggling with mental fortitude, and I continued to struggle with performance on the field. Once Grant and I started working together, he took my game to the next level. The knowledge he has in athletics (which is a great amount) is nothing compared to how much knowledge he has in the mental game and to what he can help you with to excel your play. This book is just a testament to the hard work this man has put into building his craft and his business to become his greatest self and help athletes then become their greatest selves. I am thankful for his friendship and the help he gave me, as I have taken some of these tools with me to the next level and beyond. This book is a must read and it is something that will allow for the young athlete to learn the necessary skills to succeed and for the regular human to realize the tricks of the mental game. Whether we like it or not the mental game is a huge factor in our daily lives, and there is no one better than Grant Parr to have by your side."

— **HUNTER BISHOP**

Baseball Player, Arizona State University

THE

NEXT ONE UP

MINDSET

THE
NEXT ONE UP
MINDSET

HOW TO PREPARE FOR THE UNKNOWN

GRANT PARR

Advantage®

Published by Advantage, Charleston, South Carolina.
Member of Advantage Media Group.

ADVANTAGE is a registered trademark, and the Advantage colophon is a trademark of Advantage Media Group, Inc.

Printed in the United States of America.

10 9 8 7 6 5 4 3 2 1

ISBN: 978-1-64225-076-3
LCCN: 2019937027

Book design by Jamie Wise

This publication is designed to provide accurate and authoritative information in regard to the subject matter covered. It is sold with the understanding that the publisher is not engaged in rendering legal, accounting, or other professional services. If legal advice or other expert assistance is required, the services of a competent professional person should be sought.

Advantage Media Group is proud to be a part of the Tree Neutral® program. Tree Neutral offsets the number of trees consumed in the production and printing of this book by taking proactive steps such as planting trees in direct proportion to the number of trees used to print books. To learn more about Tree Neutral, please visit **www.treeneutral.com**.

Advantage Media Group is a publisher of business, self-improvement, and professional development books and online learning. We help entrepreneurs, business leaders, and professionals share their Stories, Passion, and Knowledge to help others Learn & Grow. Do you have a manuscript or book idea that you would like us to consider for publishing? Please visit **advantagefamily.com** or call **1.866.775.1696**.

I dedicate this book to my Dad. Your unconditional love and guidance have made me the man who I am today. I wish you were here to see how your love has influenced my work of service. You're number one.

TABLE OF CONTENTS

FOREWORD

Grant Parr has been a friend, a colleague, and a supporter of my life for many years now. His passion and commitment to mental skills training is on full display with his debut book, *The Next One Up Mindset*. I am so grateful that he wrote this powerful guide; it is a beautifully written pathway to your greatness. Grant has proven to me over and over and over again that his love for helping others is genuine, real, and so necessary for the world.

I have been a mental skills coach since 2004, and to see the momentum that Grant has created over the last several years is so inspiring to me. The stigma that mental health is somehow negative is gone! Everyone now knows that mental health is important and valuable, which is an awesome thing! You can thank Grant for helping turn around this old, limited mentality into the thriving mindset of today's peak performers. Everyone now wants to train their mind. Thank you, Grant, for this amazing contribution to the overall mental health of anyone who reads your work.

I encourage you to apply what Grant is coaching here. It's a gift to be aware, and Grant will help open your mind. You then have the opportunity to practice his coaching ways. That's the key. Practice the ways of *The Next One Up Mindset* every day. Get your mental reps in. Remember there is no "perfect", just constant and diligent practice. Thank you, Grant! Thank you for this major contribution. Enjoy, everyone.

—GRAHAM BETCHART

Founder, Train the Mind

ACKNOWLEDGMENTS

First and foremost, this book couldn't have happened without the love and support of my wife, Nicole. It is your spirit and conviction for life that inspires me to do what I do. If it wasn't for my family (Dad, Mom, Joelle, and Trent), I wouldn't have a clue how to be mentally tough, gritty, or resilient. I have been fortunate to have incredible coaches, teachers/mentors, and friends that have supported me through adversity and my "unknowns." Thank you for the love, guidance, and accountability.

"YOU'RE UP, KID!"

Life has a habit of throwing things at you that you aren't prepared for. Some of life's curveballs are inevitable. But a lot we just can't see coming. Like how at thirty-six, because of injuries I had sustained over a career as an athlete—including playing football throughout college—I needed a hip replacement. Or how after that hip replacement, the doctors encountered a huge and ever-growing mass of scar tissue on my hip flexor that was so extreme they had never seen anything like it. I was the rare patient who suffered a severe case of heterotopic ossification, which is the abnormal growth of bone in the non-skeletal tissues including muscle, tendons, or other soft tissue. The new, unnatural bone grows at three times the normal rate, resulting in jagged, painful joints. It left me more crippled than before the surgery. Can anyone really be prepared for your doctor to hand you a handicapped placard for your car and tell you, "You're just going to have to be okay with being disabled"?

I have been an athlete all my life. From the age of seven, I'd been active in baseball, football, basketball, soccer, and track. In high school and college, my very identity was tied up in being an athlete. I had always possessed a warrior's mentality that was rooted in the athletic culture I cherished, a mentality I carried into my corporate job. Yet within three years of that hip replacement surgery, the lack of mobility, bone malformation, and alteration to my stride had also turned my spine in three places. When I slept, my hands would go numb. My post-surgical injuries were so severe that I couldn't clip my toenails or tie my shoes for over three years. I couldn't even use a public bathroom without my leg sticking into the adjoining stall. That's not exactly the sort of turn on life's wheel I had visualized or been prepared to meet. My warrior spirit seemed insufficient to fight through the pain and disability. How had my body let me down? How had the game I loved taken what made me *me* away?

While my body needed the help of experts to identify and treat the condition that had left me disabled, no amount of surgery could heal me unless I found the mental toughness to face the path toward healing or overcome the despair I felt at my incapacity. But, with time, desire, and support from those I love, I found strength within. I'll share the details of that story before this book is done. Mentally, I'm tougher, more flexible, healthier than I've ever been, and I've dedicated my life to helping others—athletes, businesspeople, youth—to developing the mental performance skills that allow them to achieve their dreams.

NO AMOUNT OF SURGERY COULD HEAL ME UNLESS I FOUND THE MENTAL TOUGHNESS TO FACE THE PATH TOWARD HEALING

My own path to recovery meant a return to the *me* I had discovered through the world of sport and the lessons participating on teams and against myself and opponents had taught me.

THREE LOSSES AND ONE BIG WIN: WHERE MY "NEXT ONE UP" JOURNEY BEGAN

The route of my recovery from a broken body in my thirties can be traced to a football game in my college freshman season at Chabot Junior College. I'd chosen Chabot specifically because they had made it into the national championship game the year before and the quarterback who had helped get them there had moved on.

As I entered football training camp at Chabot as a wide-eyed freshman, I was battling to be the starting quarterback with a guy from Florida who had been one of those "all-everything" players in high school and who had more high-level playing experience than I did. Our offensive coordinator liked his style of play better than mine. For the first time in my life, I wasn't starting when we opened the season against the College of the Sequoias, but I was still excited to be playing the game I loved, in college, for what I knew was a very good team. There, on a nearly one-hundred-degree night in Visalia, as my college career started with me on the bench, I remained happy as I soaked in all the excitement of a new season. Watching from the bench was completely new for me, but I had confidence in my ability. I never gave up my process. That process had got me to the college level. Football culture, from the smell of the field's cut grass to the sweat of the locker room to the feeling of comradery and adrenaline, was what I lived for.

We were playing a good team, one ranked third in the state as the season opened, but we were not executing and our quarterback could not find his rhythm. We were down 14–0 at halftime. In the locker room, the offensive coordinator found me and said, "Hey, we're gonna give you a chance, but you have a short leash."

I said, "All right," but inside I was excited and nervous as hell at the same time. When I took the field, I played a little scared, not just because of the pressure but because I had been an option quarterback and we ran a Wing-T offense. The Wing-T demands that a quarterback sacrifice his body by luring the defensive end into attacking him before he makes the pitch to his running back, and defensive ends were always looking for the chance to light me up with a heavy hit.

All my life, my friends and teammates had given me a hard time about the way I ran, saying not only could they recognize me at a distance by how I moved, but because of the swagger I knowingly exhibited. That night I operated from fear, but I had confidence in myself, and I'd learned not to show my fear. I let my fear fuel me rather than freeze me, and I'm sure I ran onto the field with my normal stride. I took the opportunity to show what I could do and I lit it up that second half. I threw two touchdowns, and at the middle of the fourth quarter, we were up 21–14. I had thrown my first touchdown pass in a college game, again experiencing that moment as a TD pass reaches your receiver's hands when joy and adrenaline and satisfaction all flood your body at once. I could sense that the other players were rallying around me. I could feel their belief in me. This was the feeling I'd been chasing as an athlete the whole time.

With less than three minutes left in the game, still up by a touchdown, we were on their forty-yard line. It was third down and we needed eight yards. Get that first down and we could eat up the clock and win the game. I was in the huddle looking to the sidelines to receive the play. The coach called a play that required two tight-ends, but I looked around my huddle and saw only one. I literally ran toward the sideline, yelling to my coach that we needed Eric Brown, the other tight-end, on the field, and while I was running, I looked down the sideline and way at the end of the bench there sat Eric with his helmet off. The play clock was running. I was screaming. After what seemed forever, the coach understood and got Eric's attention. Eric was running onto the field and I was running back to the huddle, when my coach called my name and changed the play—another with a double tight-end formation.

I sprinted into the huddle to avoid a delay-of-game penalty. I arrived frantic and out of breath. I stared at my teammates. My mind was blank. I couldn't think. I couldn't form words. Everyone in the huddle was screaming at me, "Call the play, call the play." I stared at them and I heard someone ask again, "What's the play?" I could see the play in my head, but no matter how hard I tried, I couldn't give it a name or call its number. Desperate, I said, "The two play, the two play." An offensive lineman asked, "What the f*** is a two play?" Another offensive lineman, my guard said, with an uncertain look on his face, 32 Power?"

"Yes, yes, yes," I shouted. "32 Power." I rushed the team to the line of scrimmage. In my hurry to get the play off, I committed the quarterback's cardinal sin—I didn't look to see if my running backs were set. I called the snap count, felt the ball slam into my hands, turned, and nobody was there. I was sacked for a loss of fifteen yards. All the joy, elation, satisfaction, and sense of accomplishment rushed out of my body as I was drilled into the turf.

In that moment, one that had so much riding on it, I was not prepared. I'd panicked. I'd become frantic and lost my breath. Decades later, after overcoming so much physical pain and mental anguish, I left the comfort of my career to return to school to earn a degree in sports psychology, I now possess the knowledge to recognize that there were so many things I could have done in that moment to change the way I reacted to pressure had I been prepared to face the unexpected.

But instead of being prepared when opportunity was presented,

I stumbled. I gave into panic and forgot to breathe.

We punted, and then on the first play of their series they threw a fifty-one-yard touchdown bomb. They went for the two-point conversion and got it. So, there we were, time winding down in the game and they were beating us by one point. We had enough time for one more series. I played well. Our team rallied under the pressure and drove the ball down the field. As time ran out, we had one shot at the end zone. I placed a pass just shy of the end zone, right on line for my wide receiver, and a defensive back got one hand up, just barely tipping the ball and sending it over my receiver's hands. If he'd caught it, his momentum would have carried him into the end zone and we would have won the game.

Despite the loss, a part of me walked off the field thinking, "Okay, I messed up, but you know what, I showed this team and I showed myself that I can play college football." I'd proven something to myself and was anxious for the next opportunity.

I felt good even though we lost. My offensive coordinator didn't exactly agree with my assessment of my performance. After the game and he put his arm around me and I thought that he was going to comfort me and give me some positive reinforcement. Those were the naïve thoughts of an eighteen-year-old. Instead, he literally grabbed me and pulled me in tight to him and then turned me around and pushed me up against a wall. He started jabbing his hands into my armpits, screaming at me that the loss was all my fault. When he was finished and had stormed away, I wanted to cry. But later, a number of my teammates came and talked to me and said, "Dude, you're our quarterback, man. You showed us." Their belief in me got me through the next week of practices.

Heading into the second game of the season, the offensive coordinator made it clear I would not be playing. Drawing on all my experience, despite my disappointment and frustration, I knew only one thing: I still had to get prepared. I had to be ready. The sport I loved demanded that of me. The team demanded it. I demanded it of myself. As promised by my coach, I didn't play. We lost the game 14–0.

The pattern repeated itself in week three even though they fired the offensive coordinator before the game. But then, late in the second quarter, I got the call. My head coach put me in. Eventually I learned that he had thought I was the better quarterback all along. We were losing 21–7. I entered the huddle, found my breath, and played the game I'd always loved. We clawed our way back and were beating them as the game wound down. Ultimately, we lost on a fifty-one-yard field goal with one second left. I didn't let that loss get me down, no more than I let my mistakes or my offensive coordinator's lack of belief in me keep me from preparing to seize opportunity. From that game on, I became the starting quarterback. I ended up breaking records and playing the best football of my career.

Ultimately, I thrived. But before I did, I lost my breath; I froze.

That's really the question in the end: Will you freeze or will you thrive? Will you arrive out of breath, or will you learn to inhale deeply, breathe, and find focus and confidence? In my case, a moment asking if I was ready to be the next one up arrived when I was eighteen and in a football game. Your moment might come in another sport or on the job or even at home, but such moments will, inevitably, come. You might argue that the moment that really has mattered the most for me didn't come during my freshman year, but was delayed for nearly two decades when I lived daily with a broken body and a broken spirit. That's when my resolve was truly put to the measure. Nearly two decades lost to living with pain and without a clear dream to guide me. In those years, too often I lived by looking backwards, longing for the "old Grant." I lived in daily fear. I forgot to be present in the moment, and I forgot to set new goals. I forgot to dream, and I forgot to breathe.

I'm living a new dream now. I overcame the fear. You can, too. The biggest part of my new dream is helping people just like you. And that's what this book is all about, a playbook for teaching you how to prepare yourself to respond when your number is called and you are the "next one up."

LEARNING TO BREATHE: THRIVING AS THE NEXT ONE UP

My dad was my baseball coach from the time I was seven until midway through high school. A standout player himself, he was the best coach I ever had—and the best supporter an athlete could ask for. My dad was highly sought after by teams as a coach; other coaches and players valued his knowledge, his nature, and his personality. Even as a boy, long before I really knew what he meant, he taught me and my brother many of the techniques I employ with athletes today—concepts now proven by sports psychology research—only then I didn't know their full value and they didn't have a name that I knew. Sadly, my dad passed three years ago, but I often wonder what he would say if he heard how many times a day I'm asking an athlete to focus on his or her breath.

I'm not exaggerating when I say my dad employed mental performance techniques with me and my brother nearly all our lives.

I can remember how, when we were around eleven or twelve years old, he had us listening to Rod Carew visualization/hypnosis cassette tapes. They were super cheesy. I can still remember the new age music that started them, and then out of nowhere you'd hear a bat hitting a ball repeating in ten second intervals, which would relax you and help you visualize the proper way to swing. I still use elements of these techniques with athletes today.

I guess in these regards, my dad was way ahead of his time. From an early age, he emphasized positive self-talk. He would regularly say, "You're number one!" the night before a game or in our last interaction before a game started. His statement was not that I had to be number one, but just "be number one"—strive for that, hold that belief in my mind. It was a mindset instilled in my brother and I from the time we started sports. Dad boosted our self-confidence and encouraged us to see ourselves performing at our best and becoming leaders on our teams. And he was big on the concept that is at the heart of all I do: concentrate on your breathing. My dad would always say, "If you want to control the game, you've got to control your breath."

"IF YOU WANT TO CONTROL THE GAME, YOU'VE GOT TO CONTROL YOUR BREATH."

As a mental performance coach today, I still apply my dad's lessons every time I work with an athlete or a corporate client. I get them to stop and breathe. My ultimate aim is to give them an edge by focusing on the mental game they can employ to be successful. That's what this book is about, applying the knowledge I have as a mental performance professional and the life experiences I have had as an athlete and as a businessman in order to provide you with techniques you can use when you face chaos. I offer what I've learned to help you be prepared to flourish when your number is called, and you become the next one up—a set of best practices you can apply in order to reach your peak performances. Everything in the approaches I teach in this book are transferrable into your lives. So whether you find yourself in a hard conversation with a coach or a boss, when you're in a seemingly impossible situation, when you are trying to prepare to go into a job interview or face your first start with a team that has spent a season with someone else in your role, you'll know how to gather yourself, not give into the fear and emotion, and face what's coming next.

WHY WE START WITH WHAT COMES NATURALLY: BREATHING

My dad knew something intuitively about achieving performance. His advice to focus on your breath is a great starting point, whether you are a weekend warrior or an elite competitive athlete. It is critical when facing the unknown, whether the unknown is something you've been working toward for years or arrives in your life as a complete surprise. Focusing on your breath is where this book starts and functions as a lynchpin, for within this simple concept are all the elements that can calm inner fears, erase self-doubt, and create poise: connectedness, focus, clarity, relaxation. Paying attention to your breath offers a mechanism for feeling grounded, alive, and in control. So much is beyond your control, which is all the more reason you have to "control your controllables." Focusing on taking a deep slow breath will always bring you back into the present and realign you with what is within your control. You can't compete against the last play or the next one. When your breathing is shallow and quick, your game feels tense and restricted and you will give in to the fear of those things beyond your control.

Leka Fineman, a client of mine who, in her fifties is both a CrossFit trainer and a CrossFit athlete, is a three-time NorCal Master's Champion who finished seventh in her age class in the 2017 CrossFit Games. She speaks in vivid, original ways about battling fear. She said, in an interview with me for my podcast, "It goes back to 'feeding the good wolf' and put energy toward the positive … when a negative thought comes up, you have to battle it with something positive."[1] Leka is a master at using breath to center herself and push on through adversity. Breath is vital. Just like in yoga and meditation, I will constantly be taking you back to your breath. It is something I focus on with all my clients, and they are accustomed to reciting this Breathing Commandment: I will always remember that breathing is the skill that keeps the mind calm and the body strong during adversity.

BREATHING COMMANDMENT: I WILL ALWAYS REMEMBER THAT BREATHING IS THE SKILL THAT KEEPS THE MIND CALM AND THE BODY STRONG DURING ADVERSITY.

From focused, controlled breathing we will develop ways to use other aspects of mindfulness, like visualization, positive self-talk, and positive psychology, alongside practical advice on things like goal-setting and communication approaches to help you reach your fullest potential.

This book will apply some of those concepts I first encountered as a boy playing for my father and link the science behind why these

1   Grant Parr, "Leka Fineman, CrossFit Games Master Athlete and Author," July 17, 2018 in *90% Mental,* podcast, MP3 audio.

and other mechanisms of mental performance training work so well in the way of effective application. I have drawn on all aspects of my life, from a lifetime of high-level, multi-sport athletic competition, setting records and winning accolades as a college quarterback to seventeen years excelling in corporate sales in the technology sector and then pursuing a graduate degree in sports psychology. All those parts of my life have added up to my founding of Gameface Performance, a consulting practice focused on enhancing mental skills for athletes and coaches to improve performance in sport. All of the parts of my life, even the battle against injury, have come together with the mission I strive to accomplish every day at Gameface Performance and the work I do helping others prepare to face the unknown.

Central to this book, I practice what I preach. Every technique you will encounter in *The Next One Up Mindset* is a technique I actively apply in my life and business. Mental performance training with an expert is something I wish I had in my life as an athlete. I have no doubts that I would have performed better consistently and sustained my love for the sport. That's not the case for me. I left football at the end of my junior year at Sonoma State University with a broken, failing body, sullen spirits, and riddled with self-doubt. It's been a long journey back, one in which the techniques and approaches you will encounter in this book have been the most important road signs.

Along the way, you will hear me reference all kinds of inspiring people and their stories within this book, including Bruce Lee. Because, for me, Bruce Lee, who I first encountered through my love of movies, offered the vehicle to critical mental performance training from a perspective I'd not encountered elsewhere, particularly in the Zen tradition. Indirectly it was my love of his movies that led me to first encounter the invaluable advice of the Chinese parable: "The bamboo that bends is stronger than the oak that resists." The concept is as simple as it is ancient; when a forest faces a severe windstorm, rather than remain rigid like the oak, we should "bend like bamboo." The message to us is that, in our resiliency, we do not break. At the end of my junior year, I broke. I did not always display the grit and resiliency this book will help you learn how to develop.

That came later. It came through years of fighting back through the mental hazards formed of living in a twisted, disabled body, further complicated by the tortuous hip replacement recovery I experienced in my early thirties. Years of not being able to walk without a limp, having to rediscover myself in an identity bigger than the "athlete" by which I long defined my life. I've found grit, developed mental focus, and rekindled the inner warrior that came so naturally once as an athlete. So when I say I live by the methods you will discover in this book, I am not exaggerating. Like all of you, I've known success and failure. I have fallen and gotten back up again.

Beyond my own experience and through the professional expertise I have developed in the application of mental performance techniques I learned while pursuing my graduate degree, this book will introduce you to a number of other people's stories who proved ready when asked to be the "next one up." Some of these stories will be unfamiliar to you and some will be from people so famous they've become household names. All will inspire and motivate you to reach your peak performance. They will help you discover mechanisms for winning the mental battle of overcoming fear. Many come through conversations I have had with fascinating, accomplished athletes, coaches, and mentors presented in the podcast I host: *90% Mental* (available on iTunes or Soundcloud).

Throughout the book, I address applications of these techniques for the workplace and I have included a chapter at the end of the book on how these principles can help at work, particularly at points of critical transition in your career.

There are lots of carry-overs from athletics to our workplaces. The reverse is also true, because for the career, competitive athlete— at least during their prime physical years—the game and properly preparing for it is their workplace. The ideas you will encounter in *The Next One Up Mindset* apply in all parts of your life, personally and professionally. In my own case, I was eventually forced out of high-level competitive athletics and then had to be active in developing my preparation for a career after sports—something all athletes face. What I found as I entered my first job as a recruiter in the tech sector was another culture I liked and understood. In a way, I'd traded a football jersey for another uniform, only this was white shirts and a very particular cut of suit, but I had entered another structured, competitive, enthusiastic team culture. I thrived in it, as I had in athletics. I found myself somewhere I was awarded for being competitive and in a position where I could show my leadership, enthusiasm, and teamwork skills. I accomplished quick promotions and moves to other companies and to other aspects of sales. Today, in addition to my work with athletes, I work with executives in transition, applying the concepts you will find in this book as they encounter unexpected paths in their careers.

Ultimately, what can work for executives comes down to the same thing that can increase confidence and motivation and decrease anxiety for athletes by training the mind. And that's my true love and why, after seventeen years achieving high levels of success in corporate sales, I went back to college and studied sports psychology and now focus most of my consulting on athletes. The book starts with this simple belief: athletes can't afford to rely solely on their physical talents. Athletes and coaches alike contend with internal and external factors including performance anxiety, energy/stress management, confidence issues, attention/concentration control, conflict management, season/career ending injuries, to name but some of the hurdles they face. This book focuses on a holistic, inside/out approach to enhance and improve your mental approach to your game, your career, and your life.

Connecting the mind and body to produce an elite mindset to overcome internal and external distractions while performing is vital to your success. Whether it is on the field, the court, the track, in the pool, in the performance hall, or in the office, unexpected moments will come when you are offered the opportunity to be the "next one up." This book will provide you the means not just to prepare for such a moment, but to seize it and thrive.

CHAPTER 1

"HOLY S#%T! WHAT DO YOU MEAN I HAVE TO PLAY?"

Turning Crisis into Opportunity

The ability to conquer one's self is no doubt the most precious of all things that sports bestows.

—Olga Korbut, four-time Olympic gold medalist, gymnastics

On January 26, 1992, when the Buffalo Bills offense took the field in Super Bowl XXVI, the running back who took the first handoff from Jim Kelly was not Thurman Thomas, who had won the NFL's Most Valuable Player of the Year award with over 2,000 yards from scrimmage, but back-up Kenneth Davis. Why did Thomas miss the first two plays to open the game? Because he couldn't find his helmet. It was a laughable moment, but a crisis nonetheless, and one that has infamously endured.

When Davis found himself suddenly in the next one up position, he should have served the role well—he as well had put up impressive stats that season, rushing for 624 yards as Thomas's back-up. On the first play of the game, Davis ran the play to wrong side, not giving Jim Kelly a way to hand off the ball. On the next play, he missed a block that resulted in Kelly being sacked. Davis choked when the big moment came, gaining only seventeen yards all day (though still outpacing Thomas for the game, who managed a meager thirteen yards on ten carries). The Bills went three-and-out on that first possession and went on to lose to the Washington Redskins 37–24. There's a lot of lore hidden in the cavity of that missing helmet.

Talk about being caught unprepared. For most fans, it's Thomas's helmet that gets all the attention. I'm more preoccupied with Kenneth Davis.

We are all going to face moments when, at a time of crisis, we are asked to step up. That might be in a competitive moment, like the one I faced at Chabot Junior College my freshman year, or it might come when a succession plan is suddenly put into action because of a sudden and unforeseen departure by a key executive whose shoes you are asked to fill. Will you panic? Or will you take a deep, calming breath and step into the role you have dreamed about? Are you prepared?

Even when you believe you are actively taking the proper steps toward your dreams, the path ahead will be filled with unforeseen obstacles. Your body might fail to meet the excruciating demands you make of it, or a hit you cannot control or a planted foot that twists the wrong way because of a weather-soaked field might threaten your career. Or everything in your game might be going perfectly well on the stat sheet, but something inside you is not aligning and you simply doesn't feel right. All of these are next one up moments; the next one to step up; the next moment to step into.

This book gives you a playbook for facing the unknown. It provides techniques and processes you can use when encountering the chaos of an emotional hurricane as a set of best practices. From it you will learn how to control what is controllable and find the mental space to trust your preparation to take on whatever is thrown in your path.

The first step toward a confident self when facing the unknown is to realize that for every forgotten helmet moment, there are legions of stories of those being called to step up who prove ready.

One such story involves two famous NFL quarterbacks: Drew Bledsoe and Tom Brady. Bledsoe was the first overall pick of the 1993 NFL draft, and his presence as the New England Patriots quarterback helped end a seven-season postseason drought when he led them to the playoffs four times and to Super Bowl XXXI. Looking every bit the quarterback of their future, in 2001, Bledsoe was signed by the Patriots to a then-record ten-year, $103 million contract. Yet, during the second game of the 2001 season, Bledsoe was hit by New York Jets linebacker Mo Lewis and suffered a sheared blood vessel in his chest, which almost resulted in his death.

Crisis.

Enter the now legendary Tom Brady, Bledsoe's backup, a sixth-round draft pick the year before. A player who looked like he'd been preparing for his opportunity as the next one up his whole life, Brady took Bledsoe's place in the game and performed so well he took his starting position. Although the Patriots lost that game against the Jets, with Brady assuming the helm for the remainder of the season, the team went 11–3, won the AFC East, and won the Super Bowl, with Brady becoming only the second quarterback in history to lift the Lombardi Trophy in his first season as a starter. Of course, the rest of Brady's history as a Patriot and his statistics seem nearly mythical: leading the team to six Super Bowl victories (to date) and nine appearances, four Super Bowl Most Valuable Player awards, fifteen division titles, and thirteen Pro Bowl selections. Look at his position statistics and there is no wonder most football analysts consider him one of the greatest quarterbacks to ever play the game.

But in the truest spirit of the principles of this book, that 2001 story doesn't quite end just on Brady's preparation for facing the untested terrain of success as an NFL quarterback pressed into service at a time of crisis. Though he never regained his starting role, Drew Bledsoe proved critical to his team's success and more than capable of stepping up when he replaced an injured Brady that same season in the AFC Championship game against Pittsburgh. Bledsoe, starting from the Steelers forty-yard line, capped a scoring drive with an eleven-yard touchdown pass to seal a 24–17 victory. Sometimes the next one up is found on a two-way street.

More than a great story, jumping prepared into the unknown is also a model for some of the inevitability of life. Just as most athletes are going to face moments when they are asked to step in at a time of crisis, all will have days—or seasons—of struggle, and all will face a time when they must leave the game. Your life on the job will prove nearly identical in these facets, with opportunities presented because of points of crisis—stepping up at a time of promotion, meeting shifting responsibilities, moving elsewhere to seize a new prospect, changing companies or even industries, and yes, stepping down with retirement, corporate restructuring, or job loss.

For some, there are obstacles in place that create a daily presence of such struggles, people who must create powerfully resilient minds just to compete. Consider the daily demands placed on swimmer Kathleen Baker, Olympic gold and silver medalist and current world record holder for the 100-meter backstroke. Imagine the training complications required to be the world's fastest swimmer in your event when you suffer Crohn's disease. As Kathleen discussed when I interviewed her for my podcast, everything in her life requires a difficult balance to maintain the physical demands necessary to swim at world championship pace while providing the rest and strict diet required by a chronic illness. Kathleen simply cannot always swim the same number of workouts as her teammates, and must be so finely tuned in her mind to listen to her body and rest when her Crohn's symptoms

WILL YOU ARRIVE AT A MOMENT OF CRISIS OUT OF BREATH LIKE I DID WHEN I COULDN'T FIND MY SECOND TIGHT END, OR WILL YOU MEET THE MOMENT FOCUSED, POISED, AND CONFIDENT?

are at their worst. Yet she must maintain her competitive edge, training her mind and getting the very most out of her workouts. Facing this kind of chaos everyday means developing critical mental performance habits and mental reps.

Whether you face a chronic condition like Kathleen Baker or a one-time sudden need to step up like Tom Brady, the question in all such scenarios of facing the unknown is this: Will you arrive at a moment of crisis out of breath like I did when I couldn't find my second tight end, or will you meet the moment focused, poised, and confident?

Corey Withrow, a ten-year perennial back-up center in the NFL, reinforced the need for constant preparation when I interviewed him for my podcast. Corey, undersized for the position and remarkable in his mental toughness (moving from a walk-on at Washington State to a decade in the NFL), said, "You never know when you're up. Linemen go down hurt in every game. You have to have a mindset where you prepare for the game seven days before the game begins, because you never know when you will be needed. The game moves too fast [to react without such mindful training]."[2] You don't get the luxury of easing into being the next one up. If you're not ready, the game will pass you by.

POISED, CONFIDENT, AND FOCUSED

From my junior year of high school onward and throughout the rest of my playing career, I had the habit of taping my wrists and writing, in bold black marker, the letters "P, C, F" on the tape. Those letters stand for **poised**, **confident**, and **focused**. I first got the idea from my brother's best friend, Jason Bamer, who went on to play football for the University of Hawaii, because he used to write stuff on his wrists. Jason lived right behind us throughout my childhood and even lived with us for a couple of years. I always viewed him as a mentor. He might write sayings, his number, song lyrics on his wrist tape. I respected him and wanted to emulate him. Talking one evening after practice, we came up with the idea of PCF. It became my thing. Eventually I put the acronym on the pockets of my letter jacket too. Frequently, if I found myself freaking out in a game or growing antsy on the sidelines while waiting to take the field, I'd look at my wrists, and seeing those letters would bring me back into control. They continue to be words I try to achieve in every aspect of my life and principles I try to instill in the athletes and executives

---

2   Grant Parr, "Corey Withrow—former NFL Center: CTE and Life After Football," September 11, 2018 in *90% Mental*, podcast, MP3 audio, https://podtail.com/en/podcast/90-mental/corey-withrow-former-nfl-center-cte-and-life-after/.

with whom I work. The idea behind them is a critical principle of a next one up belief system. The words have meaning and are larger than themselves.

THE NEXT ONE UP MINDSET

The attributes of those who possess a next one up mindset are:

- Prepared
- Poised
- Confident
- Focused
- Intentional

In my case, call it what you want—arrogance, naivete, stubbornness—I refused to let my college coach get to me when he wouldn't let me start. I refused to let him control what was inside my head. Maybe it's because I simply loved the game so much, loved everything about the whole culture of football, or maybe it was because I'd been picturing myself playing college football for years. I'd grown realistic over time, knew I was not the athlete who would play ball at USC, but I knew I was skilled enough to play for this very talented, nationally ranked team at Chabot. So, despite not starting, I still prepared to start. I looked at those letters written on my taped wrists, I went through my reps, I watched the starting quarterback play, I studied the playbook and cheered on my team and helped where I could help; I worked hard in practice; I bonded with teammates. I wasn't going to lose my breath the next time I got a chance to play. As you'll remember from the prologue, just before halftime of the third game, my head coach told me he was putting me in. I was ready.

Which points to another thing about sports and about life. Nothing is forever. Every time we fail is an opportunity to learn. When we are not ready to face the unknown, it is natural to want to react with fear. In some ways, the real job of mental performance training is to create a fearless mind. Withrow also told me something important about fear and mental toughness: "If you're not okay with getting knocked down, you're never going to get up. Everybody gets knocked down. How soon, how quickly you get up is what demonstrates real mental resolve."[3] If you discover you are not mentally ready to excel, well then, what do you do? You go train your mind, learn what you need to learn to get yourself ready, and find your game face.

Case in point, consider another "missing helmet" story: Dwayne Haskins. At the time of this writing, Dwayne Haskins is the sophomore starting quarterback for the Ohio State University. In 2017, a moment of crisis arrived and Haskins was asked to answer the call when, in an intense rivalry game with the University of Michigan, J.T. Barrett—then the OSU quarterback who holds the Big Ten Conference record for most passing touchdowns in a career—went out with an injury. Haskins took the field, but as he left the sideline and put on his helmet, it didn't fit—because it wasn't his helmet. He had picked up an offensive lineman's helmet by mistake. Once he found his own helmet, as he approached the line, he forgot to put in his mouthpiece. An official, seeing this, told Haskins, "I know you're nervous, son, but if you don't put your mouthpiece in place, I'm sending you back to the sideline." After overcoming his nerves and

---

3   Ibid.

his embarrassment, Haskins showed the mental toughness needed to get it together. Perhaps part of what he drew on was the realization he was living his dream; he had declared, at ten years old on his first visit to Ohio State that one day he would be their quarterback. He found his breath. He completed six of seven passes for ninety-four yards that day and secured an OSU win.

For every player like Dwayne Haskins, there are hundreds who succumb to their nerves instead. Applying the techniques of mental performance training could have allowed them different outcomes, and permitted them to draw on whatever calming, focusing mechanisms Haskins used to regain control.

THE NATURE OF FEAR

In order to step up to your dreams, living by such words like I did with PCF, breathing them in to your life is what matters as they become conduits to calming your mind and controlling your fear. A good starting point is to stand the word "fear" on its head and see it as an acronym that stands for "false evidence appearing real." A.J. Andrews, a professional softball player and the first woman to win a Rawlings Gold Glove Award, echoed this acronym when she told me in an interview, "Getting over fear is about talking to yourself. Just try it one time. One time. Once you realize nothing happened, you realize your fear is irrational, it is made up, and then you realize your power to never have to be afraid again."[4] In all competitive sports, like most of life, we need to stop concentrating on the "what ifs" and focus instead on "what can I do?" We must control what is con-

---

4   Grant Parr "A.J. Andrews - Professional Softball Player 'The Gold Glove Mindset',"
     April 21, 2018 in *90% Mental*, podcast, MP3 audio, https://podtail.com/en/
     podcast/90-mental/a-j-andrews-professional-softball-player-the-gold-/.

trollable and recognize that the flip side of fear is strategy—strategical approaches to what is within our control.

A first step in overcoming fear is to recognize 99 percent of the people we are competing against are just as nervous as we are. Your opponent is probably feeling the same emotions as you. We have to run at our fear. We can learn to embrace pressure. I interviewed Ryan Murphy—the three-time, Olympic gold medal swimmer—for my podcast, and I asked him, "What's your relationship with pressure?" His response: "I love it." If we learn to prepare and train our minds, we too can come to

IF WE LEARN TO PREPARE AND TRAIN OUR MINDS, WE TOO CAN COME TO LOVE PRESSURE AND USE IT TO OUR ADVANTAGE.

love pressure and use it to our advantage. After all, we mostly create our own pressure. Ultimately, you are competing against yourself. You are your own worst enemy and your own best ally. As Tony Robbins famously reminds us: "When you are grateful, fear disappears and abundance appears."

For similar reasons, you're not competing against the starter you hope to replace. Rather than seeing those we hope to replace as our competition, we should consciously learn all we can from how they approach their performance physically, intellectually, and mentally. As evidenced by Tom Brady and Dwayne Haskin, we should make it our habit to study those who prove their readiness. We need to pay attention to the stories of those who can show us the way to properly prepare to meet the unknown. Think what can be learned if we had the opportunity to study someone like Tua Tagovailoa, and the mindset he has demonstrated that he carries into competition. Tagovailoa, no matter what else he may accomplish in his life, will forever have earned a place among sports legends when he, as a freshman back-up quarterback, was selected by Alabama head coach Nick Sabin to take over for the second half of the 2018 National Championship game. Tagovailoa was subbed on for Jalen Hurts, who, despite having a superstar kind of season, losing only two games as a starter in two years while playing at the very highest level of college football in its dominant conference, had put in a poor performance in the first half. Alabama was down to Georgia 13–0. Everyone who knew Tagovailoa had watched how diligently he had prepared all season; they knew his readiness and talent, chief among them, his head coach. Tagovailoa, on the second possession of leading his team, tossed in a touchdown pass—on just the fifty-ninth pass of his college career. But it was the long-bomb he threw in overtime, winning the game for the Crimson Tide, that will live forever on most fans' highlight reels. Tua Tagovailoa does not throw that pass if he hadn't seen himself doing so in his imagination thousands of times before.

Of course, there is a lesson to be learned from Jalen Hurts as well, for nearly a year later, ironically, Hurts replaced an injured Tagovailoa in the SEC Championship game against Georgia, then took his team from trailing 28–21 at half to winning the game 35–28, throwing two fourth-quarter touchdowns.

Or, if you really want to understand being mentally prepared for the unknown, consider the next one up story of Mariel Zagunis. Despite being a dominant sabre fencer from the United States, Zagunis, then just nineteen, did not qualify for the 2004 Olympics, where the women's sabre event would be contested for the first time. She had more than ample credentials to belong at the elite levels of her sport, having won the Junior World Cup title three years in a row beginning in 2002, yet she had reconciled herself to watching the Olympics from the comfort of her couch. She was accustomed to being viewed as the understudy to her US Fencing teammate, Sada Jacobson, who had become the first American woman to be ranked number one in the world. Zagunis hoped to help prepare and then cheer Jacobson on to a gold medal. But then, late in the run-up to the Olympics, Nigeria decided not to send their qualifying fencer to the tournament, which opened a spot for the next highest seeded fencer in the world, Zagunis. Suddenly selected to represent the United States in the Olympics, how did Zagunis respond? She went to Athens and became the first American to win an Olympic fencing gold medal in one hundred years. Then she repeated her gold medal performance four years later. Mariel Zagunis epitomizes the spirit of being fully prepared when selected as the next one up.

Will you be prepared to turn crisis into opportunity? Are you ready to get to work?

CHAPTER 2

ROCKING THE BENCH

Embracing Your Role

There may be people that have more talent than you, but there's no excuse for anyone to work harder than you do.

—Derek Jeter, five-time World Series champion,
CEO of the Miami Marlins

At a commencement address for Barnard College, Mariel Zagunis discussed taking her teammate's place that fateful year and echoed Abby Wambach, the longtime superstar forward for the US Women's National Soccer Team, who said, "If you're not going to be a leader on the bench, how can you be a leader on the field?" Understanding and fulfilling your role as you await your opportunity is a critical aspect of truly growing prepared to make good on that opportunity.

Athletics is filled with role players. This is true in all sports, but perhaps it is nowhere more evident than in the NBA. The typical fan may only know the names of a handful of stars, but it is a league filled with defensive specialists, rebounding wizards, and three-point marksmen. It also is a league with a famous history of "sixth men," players who excel at their roles when the team needs a lift, a shift in momentum, or a defensive stop. Similarly, in a sport where the perfectly timed substitute can gain a needed goal or seal a victory, the current iteration of the US Women's National Soccer Team often features twelve women consistently ready to play at the team's elevated level.

Top bench rockers are examples of players fulfilling vital team roles and who are always ready to meet the demands and the game speed of competition requiring elite performers. Whether readying themselves to compete for a starting spot, a superstar's role, or utility presence, such athletes must be as diligent in their mental preparations to play as they are in their physical training. They must always be ready to "rock their role."

MAXIMIZE YOUR ROLE

Training the mind is every bit as important as training the body. As my mentor, Graham Betchart, a mental performance expert well known among NBA players, has written in his guide to mental performance training *Play Present*, "Repetition of your mindset creates retention of your mindset. Working on your mental game is like working on your shot. You have to practice and train daily. There is no quick fix with mental training. There is no overnight success."[5]

---

5   Graham H. Betchart and Shomari Smith, *Play Present: A Mental Skills Training Program for Basketball Players* (San Bernardino, CA, 2015).

Part of maximizing your bench role is recognizing it as a time to develop your mindset and your mental game. There's a reason an athlete must practice relentlessly to be prepared for competition. Why would the need for practice at training your mind be different than training any other part of your body? Being in "your role" is, in part, providing you the time you need to practice. No one can be ready overnight. You must train a mindset built for success.

That starts by understanding your role. You'll always have a vital one if you are smart enough to see it. Your role will be what you make of it—a launchpad for future success and a support to others while you learn, or a holding pattern leading toward stagnation and frozen development. Once you identify your role, you must embrace it. If you can learn to rock your role, you'll constantly be growing and you'll actively be helping others get better along the way. What you can't afford is an attitude that becomes "Since I'm not going to play, I'll just chill and have fun with my friends." If you're not engaged with the game from the bench, you'll never be ready to play and you certainly won't make your readiness apparent to your coaches and teammates. You need to get ready, but there's also a trust that's built up in those around you when they watch you work and see your engagement. And that attitude will become infectious; their belief in you will raise your confidence.

Charlie Batch, longtime backup quarterback for the Pittsburgh Steelers, epitomized a player who led from the bench. In a fourteen-year NFL career, all but three of them spent backing up starters, Batch's teammates consistently commented on how he represented the heart of the team, taught them to be their best, and out-hustled them every day in practice. They knew they were better and the team was better with him on it. He was the stereotype for the player who was the first one to practice, the last one to leave, and the most faithful friend and confidant on the team. We may all want to be starters, and with enough work and enough ability to see ourselves there, we may arrive at such a role, but at elite levels of sport, role players are superstars of another order inaccessible to most. Roles are not permanent, but our ability to excel at whatever our role asks of us will assure us not only that we reach our highest potential, but that we are ready to meet new roles when the opportunity is presented. For much of his career, Charlie Batch was a backup, but he was the best backup any team possessed and he earned the Super Bowl rings he owns.

ROLES ARE NOT PERMANENT, BUT OUR ABILITY TO EXCEL AT WHATEVER OUR ROLE ASKS OF US WILL ASSURE US NOT ONLY THAT WE REACH OUR HIGHEST POTENTIAL, BUT THAT WE ARE READY TO MEET NEW ROLES WHEN THE OPPORTUNITY IS PRESENTED.

Sometimes, athletes possess all the physical skills and sufficient experience to become a leader, but do not know if they are ready to assume a new role. Sometimes they must be led to that advanced role by others, including their coaches. Duke men's basketball coach, Mike Krzyzewski, detailed such a case regarding Shane Battier in a June 16, 2011 editorial he wrote about motivation for *The Wall Street Journal*. Duke had lost to Connecticut in the national championship game in the 1999 season, a team on which Battier had played an important supporting role. Several of Duke's top players left early for the NBA and Coach K needed Battier to step up, take a leadership role, and become a star, something Battier never imagined seeing himself as. Here's how Krzyzewski described how he approached his player:

After the players had gone home for the summer, I gave Shane a call.

"Shane," I said, "this morning, did you look in the mirror and imagine that you were looking at next year's conference player of the year?"

He chuckled, "Coach, I … "

I hung up.

The next day I called again. "Shane, it's Coach. When you were on your way to work this morning, did you imagine scoring thirty points in a game this season?"

He laughed cautiously and began to respond before I hung up again.

Seconds later, my phone rang. "Coach," Shane said, "Don't hang up on me."

"I won't hang up on you if you won't hang up on you," I told him.[6]

Krzyzewski goes on to explain that Battier needed to imagine what he asked of him in order to become the player that he could be. Krzyzewski explains, Battier "had all of the tools necessary to become a great player, but he fully realized his potential only when he allowed himself to imagine great things." Two years later, Shane Battier led Duke to the national championship before earning nearly every honor the NCAA can bestow on a player and being picked in the first round of the NBA draft. Battier was asked to change his role and that

---

6   Mike Krzyzewski, "Coach K on How to Connect," *The Wall Street Journal*, July 16, 2011, https://www.wsj.com/articles/SB1000142405270230367870457644182313 0334218.

meant changing how he saw himself. "For motivating Shane," Coach K explains, "the crucial word to communicate was 'imagination.' For others, it may be 'enthusiasm' or 'self-confidence' or 'poise.'"[7]

As Olympian Mariel Zagunis also suggests, you must be willing to become a leader even if your role is not presently the one at the center of the action. This starts with learning to "play" the game from the sidelines, which means being fully engaged in the competition. In the best environments, it also means talking with your teammates and sharing with them what you've seen from your point of view. You are in an ideal position to study what is happening within the action that the "starters" may not be able to focus on. Not only can this help your team and your teammate, there is a direct benefit to you and your development.

One of the difficulties of being on the bench is that you don't have the opportunity to get in game-speed reps. You don't get as many touches on the ball or with the sword, as many dives or vaults, so it is vital that you complete just as many "mental reps" as the starters. In many competitive settings, being suddenly introduced into a game already in motion is like trying to jump in the open window of a passing car going seventy-five miles-per-hour. That can be a nearly impossible adjustment, particularly if you're not regularly given the chance for reps at game speed. You've got to make up the difference in the most productive way possible, using powerful visualization techniques to place yourself inside the competition and see the decisions you would make (which might be different than those you are witnessing in others), see yourself performing and feel your body reacting to that performance.

---

7   Ibid.

HOW TO ROCK THE BENCH:

- Visualize: get in your mental reps and visualize your performance and attaining your goals.

- Study the Best: watch, listen, and read the advice and experiences of those who have excelled at what they do.

- Set Smart Goals: set attainable goals, visualize them, and develop a specific plan for reaching them.

- Be a Leader: lead from the bench by communicating with your teammates, leading by example, and going the extra mile.

- Embrace the Struggle: put in the hard work and enjoy the path toward success.

There is another aspect of the mental training that comes while on the bench that is equally important and can contribute to the leadership Zagunis speaks about, and that is becoming game-savvy. You must grow your knowledge of your sport and study the game with such detail that you understand everything about it, including its patterns and strategies, your team's plays, and your opponent's. Be a student of the game. If you are, when your number is called, you will have a larger arsenal to draw upon as you move into competition. You'll be a step up from those others who don't master their roles. Your separation is your preparation.

If you learn Zagunis's story before she was called up to the Olympic team, what you find is an athlete who studied and studied, always focusing on how to get better. Now this trait obviously carries over throughout our lives. Even when you think you are miles down the seniority ladder or years away from vying for a promotion, are you actively educating yourself about your role, your job, your company's processes and products? Are you gaining the education that not only will land you greater responsibilities, but allow you to excel once you take them on?

SETTING AND ACHIEVING GOALS: GOAL GETTING

When I think about the roles we play and their relationship to leadership, I can't help but think of a young man I helped coach in football at the high school level. He was senior and a second-string free safety, but he had been elected captain because the dude simply had a such a great attitude, showing up before anyone else and working harder than his teammates. He wasn't a bad player, he just wasn't better than the starting free safety. He took his leadership role seriously and led by work ethic and by showing greater spirit than anyone. To take on a role the way he did, to be a vocal leader even when you are not a starter, takes both courage and vulnerability.

Taking vulnerability to a whole new level, this young player also was willing to heed my advice and set a very specific goal—his was to start in at least one game. Now this sounds like a goal that is obtainable enough, until we recognize the only thing he could control was himself, his practice, his preparedness—he would still be dependent on a coach to realize the value of his goal. Setting goals is essential to fulfilling your role because part of fulfilling your role is finding achievable ways to step beyond it. And your goals should be changing over the course of time. They should be growing as you achieve them and you should be creating new ones. Critically, you need to be willing to share those goals with others, to tell your friends and family, coaches and bosses about them so that there will be someone else out there who will help hold you accountable. Without accountability, goals are meaningless.

Working with this athlete, he set his sights on starting a game, visualized himself doing so and how he would react to the pressure, put in his reps—physical and mental—so he'd be ready. And he shared his goal with his defensive coordinator. Now that coach came to me and said, "Really, you're having my second stringers ask for playing time?" I replied, "Hell yeah, I am. Don't you want your guys to ask for a promotion? Don't you want them to fight for that next step, to be hungry for it? Don't you want this young man, when he grows up and faces life beyond football, to have the courage to go get what he wants?" To his credit, the coach listened to his player and started him. And the player, well, he was incredible. In fact, because they were smoking their opponents by 44–0, the coach pulled the kid out and put in a substitute. Now how cool was it for this kid to be pulled out of a game *because* he was doing so well they needed to show their opponent a little mercy?

How you approach your goals matters. Not only do you need to share them, you need to write them down. When you do, while it's fine to write out the task-oriented needs of accomplishing that goal, you also need to mentally prepare for the goal and spend considerable energy on *seeing* and *feeling* what it will be like when that goal is attained. Create a clear, vivid picture of what your goal looks and feels like. The questions to ask yourself are: "How will I know when I achieve my goals? How will I not?" We must exhibit certainty on the things that will derail, demotivate, and distract us from our goals, so that when they appear we are prepared to manage them and stay on track. You have to see the film of it in your mind. When you do, once that goal is reached, you'll know it because you've already experienced it—its sights, sounds, feelings—in your mind. You're prepared to move forward toward it then.

While I truly am asking you to visualize the attainment of your goals, they must be attainable, actionable targets, for then you can match the mental preparedness of accomplishing them with the framework for carrying them out. There are numerous goal-building models, but the one I use most when working with athletes and others is SMART (specific, measurable, attainable, realistic, timely). Let's say you are a gymnast. You know you're solid on floor, confident in vault, improving at uneven bars, and certain you will continue to improve, but sick with worry over repeated frustrations on beam. Rather than creating a goal of a specific final beam score or a medal position, a SMART approach might be to add one specific element to your routine that bumps your difficulty score from 2.6 to 2.8 and give yourself a set number of weeks to obtain regular performance of the new element within your routine. The new element, while demanding and pushing you to improve, should link components you have the skills to complete. Now you've got a goal that's specific and measurable, one that is realistically obtainable to your skills, point of development, and to your specific schedule for accomplishing it. Once there, you raise the stakes again.

Will attaining this goal be easy? Not if it is a goal worth reaching. Which is why part of embracing your current role is all about embracing the struggle. You're working toward something. You are preparing for the unknown. That takes diligence, work, and commitment.

CHAPTER 3

SHARPENING THE AXE

Discovering Confidence in Preparation

Spectacular achievements are always preceded
by unspectacular preparation.

—*Roger Staubach, two-time Super Bowl champion*

When you think you are prepared, go prepare some more. The superstar athletes and CEOs you admire, those musicians that leave you in amazement, all got to where they are by out-preparing everyone else around them. They put in the reps; practiced after practice was over, the lesson had ended, or the workday was complete and the others had gone home; studied the playbooks by flashlight after lights-out. They learned more than would be needed to pass the test. They made conscious and conscientious decisions. If you want to grow confident in your abilities and be ready to step up when the opportunity comes, you've got to put in the work. Abraham Lincoln famously once said, "Give me six hours to chop down a tree, and I will spend the first four hours sharpening the axe."

As we've already discussed, when receiving the call to face the unknown or learning how to excel at the role assigned to you, you never know when the preparation demanded of you will be required to convert to performance. You just don't know when opportunity will strike and, because you don't, your only choice is to always be ready for it. Consider the story of Andre Ingram. In 2018, Ingram signed with the Los Angeles Lakers for the final two games of the season. In his first outing, he scored nineteen points. Ingram was thirty-two years old, notably making him the oldest American rookie in the NBA since 1964. He had been playing in the NBA developmental "G" League since 2007. Ingram proved he had the mental preparation to thrive when, after eleven years, he became an overnight sensation. He had put in the reps for eleven years.

Parts of Ingram's story, though his Laker's career only lasted two games, is similar to the 2012 phenomena you likely remember as "Linsanity." Jeremy Lin was the unlikeliest of heroes to turn around the 2012 season for the floundering New York Knicks. He played his college career at Harvard (not exactly the hotbed for NBA recruiting), was passed over in the 2010 NBA draft and brought into the NBA only after saving himself by playing well in the summer league. Then he was traded around until signed by the Warriors where he played far more frequently on their G-league affiliate in Reno than for the parent club in Oakland. Waived by Golden State, he played briefly in China, then was picked up by the Rockets only to be waived again within weeks. That's when the Knicks signed him mostly because they were so thin at guard due to injuries, and placed him fourth on the point guard depth chart. Lin stated that he was "competing for a backup spot," adding that people saw him "as the twelfth to fifteenth guy on the roster." But Lin was the kind of player who arrived first at practice and left last, intensely studying game film and working with coaches to improve his footwork and judgment. He approached his opportunity with the Knicks in the same way he had spent the 2011 off-season, diligently working to improve his jump shot by abandoning the shooting form he had used since the eighth grade and adding muscle weight. Yet he still spent his first month with the Knicks' organization relegated to their G-league team in Erie.

The Knicks were struggling, having lost eleven of their last thirteen games, and were riddled with injured players. In an early February game where the Knicks had squandered a lead against the Celtics and looked lifeless and destined to lose, coach Mike D'Antoni, in desperation, put Lin in the game, and he led them to a victory. The following night, against the Nets, coming off the bench again, Lin produced twenty-five points, five rebounds, and seven assists—all career highs. His performance continued in similar fashion over the next week, and six nights later, he set a new career high, scoring thirty-eight points in a win over the Lakers. In the press conference after that game, Kobe Bryant said, discussing Lin, "Players playing that well don't usually come out of nowhere. It seems like they come out of nowhere, but if you can go back and look, his skill level was probably there from the beginning." Bryant, the poster-child for game preparation, knew the work required to pull off the kinds of performances Lin was demonstrating. With continued strong performances from the bench that displayed the work he had so faithfully put in, Lin shifted to a starting role, and in his twelve starts before the All-Star break, Lin averaged 22.5 points and 8.7 assists, and the team had a 9–3 record.

Professional sports are loaded with stories of players like Lin and Ingram. In their cases, the kinds of success they demonstrated didn't necessarily result in longevity or sustained superstar status (although Lin, despite numerous injuries, continues to play in the NBA), but their ability to reach the highest stage of the sport speaks to the value of mental preparation and commitment to having a winning mindset. How many people can be thrust into the pressure and resulting scrutiny of a league as elite as the NBA and, rather than freeze, excel? Preparation increases confidence and motivation, while decreases anxiety and stress. Preparation is all

PREPARATION INCREASES CONFIDENCE AND MOTIVATION, WHILE DECREASES ANXIETY AND STRESS.

about focusing on the process. It bears repeating: your separation is in your preparation. You don't get to control winning, no more than Lin or Ingram could control who didn't draft them or the environments of the struggling teams on which they were placed. Graham Betchart, the mentor and mental performance expert I introduced earlier, has outstanding advice on this front when in *Play Present* he says, "Don't try to be perfect at results. Free yourself from that restrictive mindset and be perfect at your process—because that is what you control.[8]"

DIAL IN YOUR PROCESS

Lin and Ingram put in the work; they acted on their process. They had been very conscious and purposeful in developing their physical game. They were experienced and grew from that experience. But

---

8   Graham H. Betchart and Shomari Smith, *Play Present: A Mental Skills Training Program for Basketball Players* (San Bernardino, CA, 2015).

they were also mentally ready, or they could not have performed in arenas filled with 50,000 fans and national television audiences if they weren't. This is why mental preparation has to parallel physical preparation. It's normal for athletes to create, over time, practice and warm-up regimens they employ to help be prepared. We must do the same and develop mental processes.

One aspect of the importance of mental performance training is that those patterns of physical processes can frequently get interrupted or challenged by environment, circumstance, or injury. Superstition cannot substitute for process. It's okay to believe in something strongly, to establish rituals for you that help you get in the competitive mindset. But process is bigger and more adaptable than your rituals precisely because you need to retain a confident attitude and strong mental preparedness even if your process gets knocked off track. For example, when I interviewed Jeff Reed, who was a longtime placekicker for the Steelers, he told me how every time he left the locker room after halftime, he put a brand-new sock on his right foot because he viewed every half as a separate game. He said, "That game was over in the first half, so I needed a fresh foot."[9] But, and this is key, he never became so dependent on this ritual that its absence would alter his performance. So, if you have an established habit of listening to certain music to pump yourself up before a game, that can be a great tool, but your mental preparation must be rich enough, flexible enough, focused enough that if your phone dies or your headphones break, your concentration isn't lost or your positive-minded attitude is not affected.

---

9   Grant Parr "Jeff Reed, 2x Super Bowl Champion 'The Mindset of a Kicker'," November 27, 2018 in *90% Mental*, podcast, MP3 audio, https://www.gamefaceperformance.com/2018/04/21/ episode-32-a-j-andrews-professional-softball-player-the-gold-glove-mindset.

USING MUSIC AS PART OF YOUR PREPARATION

Music can be a powerful motivational tool, as well as an effective relaxation tool and can be used to aid your preparation. For me, as an athlete and a coach, music has been the soundtrack of my life. It shapes how I move in this world. It motivates me; it guides me; it grounds me; it relaxes me. I am a highly kinesthetic and auditory learner, so music resonates for me. It always has. And I have been a musician most of my life as well. Music is a common tool for lots of athletes. We've all seen athletes streaming off a team bus with headphones on, and we've seen images of athletes warming up while they move to the beat of their favorite playlist. Many of you will recall the now famous image of Michael Phelps published in *The Wall Street Journal*, sitting with his headphones on, warm-up coat hood pulled up, hands in his pockets, downcast eyes, with a stern, almost angry look on his face as he concentrates in preparation for his next event. The look on his face is so intense, he took a great deal of heat for it, and I think of that picture each time I think of my company name, Gameface Performance. Phelps has always used music as part of his preparation.

Music is a very personal and powerful thing. It can do tremendous things to shape the mind, and many of us feel extremely motivated by certain songs and rhythm patterns. There's a reason most teams have songs the players have chosen to play when they enter competition, songs that convey how they see themselves as a team, that convey their team goals, and that match the emotion they wish to apply in their performance. I always think of it this way, if you were to watch the very first *Rocky* movie without music, it may not feel like that great of a movie. It's an inspiring, motivating soundtrack. In fact, I often ask the athletes I coach, "What's your *Rocky* song?"

In my own case, I listen to good, hard-hitting heavy rock to pump me up before a performance or a speech and I use expansive, innovative music that I find calming and focusing when I meditate. Music is a very personal choice, and you should use the music that works for you, whatever that may be, or not use it at all if that's your preference. If you do use music for preparation, it's all about tapping into its energy and allowing the motions you need in the moment to flood into your mind.

BE AN MVP

Flexibility in your mental preparation is possible if you use key aspects of training in your mental game. These aspects are rooted in a sports acronym that is widely used throughout sports psychology—MVPs—Meditation, Visualization, and Positive affirmations (or what I often refer to as positive self-talk). You must practice these MVPs with as much dedication as you do any other part of your preparation. MVPs connect the mind and the body. If you make them a daily part of your process, they will be another tool with which to sharpen your axe. If you do your daily MVPs, you will become your own most valuable player, and who wouldn't want to be their own MVP of their process? As you build and strengthen the bridge between the mind and the body, you will learn to trust your skills. Doing so allows your body to perform as it has been trained to do regardless of how you feel on a given day or during a given play. Once you come to accept that you can trust your body and have conviction in your physical preparation, you will enter competition confident and motivated. Just as we have developed confidence that our bodies are going to serve us well, we grow confident in our ability to perform. That prepares us to no longer second guess ourselves in the moment. We're going to trust on the subconscious mind to do its thing because we've trained it to guide us.

> **AS YOU BUILD AND STRENGTHEN THE BRIDGE BETWEEN THE MIND AND THE BODY, YOU WILL LEARN TO TRUST YOUR SKILLS. DOING SO ALLOWS YOUR BODY TO PERFORM AS IT HAS BEEN TRAINED TO DO REGARDLESS OF HOW YOU FEEL ON A GIVEN DAY OR DURING A GIVEN PLAY.**

Long before I knew MVP as an acronym, long before I applied its principles with consciousness, I often practiced its core notions. Perhaps this was by my own instinct or maybe it was because of having good coaches and good role models—my dad included—but I had developed the habit that every time I'd break the huddle and walk to the center, I saw myself complete the play we were about to run. I'd see the play develop as it was drawn up and see myself performing my role within it. Once I had that rapid visualization, I didn't even think about the play, I just received the ball in my hand, and I turned. That's how preparation is supposed to work: you are so prepared to meet the moment that when it arrives, you simply embrace the moment. Because it is so central to so much of what you need to reach your peak performance, we'll dig into the MVP process with more depth in the next chapter.

As we develop a mental preparation process, one that incorporates the MVPs and is aimed at producing the kind of mindful moment I experienced as I approached the line of scrimmage, here are some other elements we must include if we are to succeed in reaching the highest levels of performance. These come from Justin Su'a, a mental performance coach for the Tampa Bay Devil Rays and the Cleveland Browns and host of the podcast *Increase Your Impact*:[10]

1. Win the morning.

2. Do hard things.

3. Embrace feedback.

4. Learn from failure.

5. Choose your attitude.

6. Do one more.

7. Live on purpose, with purpose.

8. Recommit every day.

9. Be patient.

10. Fear no one.

---

10 Justin Su'a (@Justinsua), "10 High Performance Habits," Twitter, March 3, 2018, https://twitter.com/Justinsua/status/969919072086515718.

Give thought to each of the items on this list Su'a has developed. Part of your preparation is about choice—choosing to embrace each day and each opportunity with an attitude that is affirming and focused on tackling difficulty head-on, listening to those around you and learning from the days that threaten to beat you, realizing that you are your own most demanding competitor, setting goals and reaffirming your commitment to achieving them, while living fully in the moment. What Su'a asks us to do must become habits, the stuff of our daily process as much as the reps in the weight room or the practice facility.

Practice each of these choices. Then practice some more. That's what's preparation is all about, within the mind, on the field, and through the body.

CHAPTER 4

A DEVIL ON ONE SHOULDER ...

Quieting the Inner Critic

Baseball is 90 percent mental and the other half is physical.

—*Yogi Berra*

When an athlete doesn't get a lot of practice or opportunities, or a professional rarely gets selected to present in front of colleagues/lead the company's new initiatives, the mind can get lonely and focus on the wrong things. Typically, these "wrong" things are out of their control. We risk giving our attention to thoughts that can eat away at us, destroy our confidence, and take us out of our rhythm; we begin to listen to a cartoon version of the devil who sits on one shoulder and whispers in our ear.

So how do we create ways to listen to that other voice within us, that angel on the opposite shoulder to quiet the inner critic? Good mental performance training provides you processes and techniques that allow you to focus on the things you can control. The foundation for all mental skills training is mindfulness, which always starts with breathing and centers on being where your feet are and living within your skin. From there, the processes you use must become purposeful and intentional. Whether applying the tools we'll develop in this chapter in practice, in competition, or in the workplace, you are creating a mindset. And if you don't have an intention, it's hard to have a mindset.

WIN IN THE PRESENT

All the processes that I will introduce you to in *The Next One Up Mindset* include learning to live within the WIN mentality—What's Important Now? I'm constantly telling athletes and corporate athletes alike, "Let's focus on right now." What does that really mean? One of the biggest risks in competitive settings where the speed of play, or the speed of and amount of decision-making required of you can feel overwhelming is to fall outside of the time that matters, the "NOW."

The Dalai Lama says, "There are two days that you don't want to live in, yesterday and tomorrow." It's too easy, particularly if you've just made a mistake or you've had a play fall apart, or you've come up short on a time goal, to dwell on that failure. But the game, like most of life, doesn't wait for you. You are required to perform right now.

There can be an equal risk, particularly after a moment when you have questioned your performance, to try and investigate the future, to think ahead to the next play or the next parry when the moment requires you to be so sharp and so focused that you act instead of think. Too much thinking about what comes next tends to create doubt. It sows the seeds of fear. You begin to think, "I just screwed up, what if I do again?" Instead, you must ask, "What's important now?" The WIN mindset is rooted in the very essence of mindfulness. It asks us to transform our thinking about the "next." Too often we dwell on what's "about to happen" as something to be thought about, analyzed, feared, or overly anticipated.

YOU'VE DONE WHAT'S REQUIRED OF YOU "NEXT" COUNTLESS TIMES IN PRACTICE, REGULARLY IN COMPETITION, AND IF YOU APPLY ALL THE PROCESSES OF THIS CHAPTER, MILLIONS OF TIMES IN YOUR HEAD. YOU'RE READY FOR "WHAT'S NEXT."

Mindfulness is filled with subtle but important distinctions. For example, the mindful athlete focuses on preparation, as we've discussed, and visualization, as we'll continue to discuss in detail, not anticipation. The distinction matters. As does this one: to reach peak performance, rather than dwelling on "What's next" and focus on the unknown (which is, by definition, unknowable), you have to create a mindset that says, "Okay, that play/race/round is over. So what? Next time bring it on." There's a difference at looking at what's next is going to be like, versus visualizing what you're going to do.

Just as there is so much we do to prepare for a performance that gets "locked in," there's a lot that happens within action that causes us to get "locked out." We can get locked out of focus. We get locked out of our bodies. So how do we learn how to get locked back in? You've done what's required of you "next" countless times in practice, regularly in competition, and if you apply all the processes of this chapter, millions of times in your head. You're ready for "what's next." You learn to become grounded in the now so that you can face the future. You just need the tools to meet the "next."

Think of the NFL placekickers for your favorite team. How often have you seen a kicker with a long career calmly step up and nail a game winner? If you're a fan, then inevitably you've seen that same kicker miss a field goal, shrug it off, and later in the same game, nail one from further out. Because of the pressure involved—from himself, from the situation, from not wanting to disappoint the team or fans—it's impossible to shrug off a miss and come back and deliver the next time you're needed unless you have a WIN mindset.

We see it in every sport in every competition—the keeper for your favorite soccer club shrugs off an allowed goal to come back and make a spectacular save minutes later; the skater who misses a triple axel performs another, flawlessly, within seconds; the tennis player double faults and follows it with an ace. They don't bounce back unless they have developed the tools that allow them to rapidly refocus and face the *now*.

WIN is exhibited in the ER doctor as she calmly prioritizes and directs immediate next actions for a critically injured patient. We see it in the team leader who, at the outset of a hectic final week before a looming project deadline, tells his team, "Here's what must be done today. Tomorrow we'll tackle tomorrow." We realize its importance when the unexpected lands in our laps—the system crashes, the power goes out, the storm threatens—and someone steps up and says, "Okay, well the next step we've got to take is …" It's more than knowing what needs to happen next, it's resetting the focus and acting on that next.

in particular, athletic competition is filled with gaps. Gaps include everything from those momentary breaks in play to the grueling anticipation that comes with down time between races or events. Dependent upon the sport and on the situation, sometimes those gaps are miniscule—racing down the court after a rebound in transition from defense to offense, stepping away after throwing a counter-punch in reaction to a flurry from our opponent. And sometimes, those gaps are substantial—the walk between holes on the golf course, halftime in a game, the wait between races. Long gaps before reentering action or short ones, both require techniques to apply the WIN mindset.

WIN starts with consciousness and commitment. With intention. A WIN mindset is every bit as important for the next one up as it is for the superstar starter, because WIN is developed on the bench, in the weight room, during practice, and within your mind. It's built from mental reps. You are shaping the mind to conceive of time differently, and you're developing tools that allow you to refocus and act.

BVT TO BE IN CONTROL

In order to respond to what comes *next* in the way that you need to be successful, you must have created processes that allow your mind to complete this refocus rapidly. The process I teach and use in my own life is BVT—Breathe, Visualize, Talk. These essential three steps, practiced so regularly they become second nature, form a process that acts as a cue that gives you a shortcut to operating in the WIN and executing performance. BVT allows you to focus on three things that you can control. No one else can control them. Control is all about a purposeful response to an emotional hurricane. In the heat of action, it's easy to feel like a storm is whirling around and inside of you. It can feel chaotic and overpowering. When you breathe, visualize your performance, and talk yourself into a positive direction, you reassert control.

B **BREATHE**

V **VISUALIZE**

T **TALK**

BREATHE

Refocusing always starts with your breath. Breathe, get grounded, be where your feet are. Be in the here and now. If you don't have your breath, you're going to be scattered and unfocused. You give into distractions. In big-time sports, there are both external distractions (the noise of the crowd, the music between batters, the pre-game press) and internal ones ("What if I forget that new play?" "I'm still sore from the last game." "We've got key injuries, so do I have to carry more than my weight or will someone new step up?"). In life, there are distractions outside of work (family, finances, relationships) and inside (problematic peers or employees, missed earning targets, new systems or personnel). The world is filled with distractions. We need a tool to get back inside the moment and block them. We need focus.

Getting in focus essentially allows you to be yourself. You're prepared for this moment. You are already breathing, but now you focus quickly on it, and by doing so, you control your breath, and in turn, you control yourself.

The specifics of how you focus your breath don't matter nearly as much as finding what works for you. I want that breath to be comfortable for you. Only you should dictate how long that takes, how many breaths you take, or how deep they are. If you want to take two big, massive inhales and then exhale, great. If it's just one big one, or just a couple short ones, cool. You simply need to practice whatever's comfortable for you, whatever allows you to start the BVT process. Ultimately, you're training your subconscious mind how to use breath to settle you.

VISUALIZE

To reach peak performance, you must be able to see yourself performing. I mean this in the most literal sense. The more precisely you can see yourself in action, the more you are able to adjust and control that image, change its details, and guide its outcome. Visualization is an exercise in concentration. You get the opportunity to control the controllable and see yourself doing the right things or correcting yourself in the moment. Like all parts of performance, visualization is something that must be practiced. You have to become comfortable in creating visualized images that doing so becomes second nature. When you control that image, you become your own filmmaker. You can slow that film down or speed it up. You get to decide whether you see that image from within or from outside your body. You get to control your approach, which is exactly the point because you are visualizing it to gain control in the moment. Whatever approach you take is fine, so long as you see yourself and emerge from the image knowing how you see yourself performing.

The goal is that the moment you emerge from the visualization of BVT, you reenter your body, you cement the image with positive self-talk, and boom, you're right back in your body and the competition. There might not be time for it as you sprint down the court in transition from defense to offense, but there certainly is during a time-out, or at the free-throw line.

For me, when I am visualizing, I'm also tapping into an emotion, feeling the confidence of the moment and for me, the joy of performing. I've written earlier about my love for the larger culture of the game—the teamwork, the excitement, all the colors and tastes and smells—and that carries into the feeling I have when visualizing competing. It's important to incorporate all these emotions together with all of your senses. The richer your sensory acuity when visualizing, the better; such that you incorporate sights, smells, sounds, and touch to form a fuller, richer picture of your actions. This is the sort of visualization of the prototypical Zen archer becoming one with the target, the act of imagining the arrow piercing the center of the target is as important as the act of releasing the arrow. We are accustomed to seeing such visualization in action when basketball players are trained to shoot an imaginary free-throw, seeing the ball go through the rim without moving the net before shooting the actual foul shot. Or we have observed visualization in process when the gymnast, the figure skater, or the Olympic diver move through the whole of a routine in a warm-up area.

For Olympic skier Emily Cook, her pre-competition routine

THE RICHER YOUR SENSORY ACUITY WHEN VISUALIZING, THE BETTER; SUCH THAT YOU INCORPORATE SIGHTS, SMELLS, SOUNDS, AND TOUCH TO FORM A FULLER, RICHER PICTURE OF YOUR ACTIONS.

goes deep inside sensory visualization. "You have to smell it," Cook said in an interview for *The New York Times* in 2014. "You have to hear it. You have to feel it, everything."[11] By imagining the smell of the snow, the roar of the crowd, and her muscles firing, Cook increases her focus and confidence while executing high-skilled, freestyle-skiing sequences.

Cook's example parallels that of Olympic gold medalist rower, Susan Francia, who told me when I interviewed her for my podcast how their coach would use step by step visualization with the entire rowing team. They could be in a hotel room the night before a race and the coach would have the team gather, sit in the positions they occupied in the boat, turn off the lights, and she would walk them through the entire race from placing their hands on their oars to each segment of the competition.[12]

Visualization can be used well beyond these rehearsed moments or the static ones, and applied as effectively to the tiniest gaps in game play when approaching the huddle or stepping to the batter's box or to the baseline before a serve. We can use the same technique before making a speech or entering the meeting or sitting for a job interview. Visualize the action you intend and you are already a step closer to a positive outcome.

For example, if I'm speaking in public, I visualize myself relaxed and confident, enjoying the interaction with audience members. My approach is to see myself presenting on the stage and feel the details of the performance and the reception. It's not significantly different

---

11   Christopher Clarey, "Olympians Use Imagery as Mental Training," *The New York Times,* February 22, 2014, https://www.nytimes.com/2014/02/23/sports/olympics/olympians-use-imagery-as-mental-training.html.

12   Grant Parr "Susan Francia—2x Gold Medalist Women's Rowing—Olympic Mindset—," May 24, 2018 in *90% Mental*, podcast, MP3 audio, https://podtail.com/en/podcast/90-mental/susan-francia-2x-gold-medalist-women-s-rowing-olym/.

from when I am working out in the weight room and completing bench presses, something I've been doing my whole life, yet I still see myself in my body, can see my arms going up and observe my form. Such visualization is empowering.

VISUALIZATION:
SEE IT. FEEL IT. DO IT!

Certified mental skills professional for the Chicago Cubs and former all-star player and author of *Ninety Percent Mental*, Bob Tewksbury, writes about working with the Chicago Cubs pitcher, John Lester, when they were both with the Boston Red Sox. Like a lot of players, Lester struggled to buy into the importance of mental performance techniques, but was looking for an edge in his game. Tewksbury literally walked Lester through a visualization of every pitch from a couple innings of a game and Lester began to see its transformative power. Now part of Lester's pregame warm-up ritual is to use the Cub's sleep room where he listens to a personalized visualization tape Tewksbury has made for him.

Anyone can learn visualization techniques, it simply takes concentration and practice. While most effectively learned with the help of a coach who can walk you through some first visualizations, most of the keys of effective practices parallel the positivity that guides what we apply when using positive self-talk, for you to consciously create vivid moving pictures of yourself completing the actions required of you in a confident, poised, and calm manner.

GUIDELINES FOR VISUALIZATION:

- Control the image; own it.

- Create images that are positive, vivid, and clear.

- Never end a visualization session on a negative experience or image.

- Strive for perfection in your images. (I don't believe in perfection; the exception is when coaching visualization because we are training the subconscious mind to do things right, under control, while staying positive.)

TALK

Call it what you want—constructive affirmations, mantras, self-talk, positive psychology—but a key part of creating productive refocusing devices is learning to become your own best motivator through the power of positive language directed at the self. Such self-talk can become the cue that moves the BVT process into the action of the next moment of performance. Whether it's as simple as saying "Go!" in your head or "I've got this!" the use of such talk completes the BVT process and sparks the body to take the actions that it has completed (and you have visualized) thousands upon thousands of times before during practice.

What we want to do with positive self-talk is create a language for ourselves, an inventory that feels good. We want to develop a language that develops purposeful optimism. The self-talk that takes place in the gaps of competition or in the brief moments immediately before taking action builds upon a far more developed language that we will discuss in the next section when we explore the process of MVP. It's important to learn how to talk yourself into a positive direction, because I have seen too many times where athletes or performers listen to their thoughts rather than talking to them. Don't allow the inner-critic to take over your voice.

PUTTING BVT TOGETHER

When first learning the BVT process, it's important to break it down, learn it step by step. First, you must learn how to concentrate on your breath. When I start working with an athlete or a team, I often begin with a thirty-minute training session focused on breathing where we draw purposefully on certain situations they regularly encounter in their performance. For example, if I'm working with a basketball player, I create situations they find familiar, like when they're in the third period, they've played twenty minutes of a tight, physical game. They're tired, breathing hard and have just come off a fast break when they've been fouled. So now they're on the free throw line. How do they stop, take that moment, and breathe?

By getting into your breath, you will have control of your mind, and if you have control of your mind, you will have control of your body, which will allow you to make the best decision with your body. Breath, mind, body ... if you don't access your breath, this process breaks down and you will feel tense, rushed, and unsound. This opens the door to the inner-critic and results in poor decisions and mistakes.

If I can get someone to learn how to ground themselves with taking a slow, conscious breath or two, if they can get comfortable and confident with that, then they can learn the next step, so that player at the free-throw line can then, after taking a breath, close her eyes for a moment and see herself completing the shot with perfect form.

BVT is a process. If, ultimately, you only use one technique out of this process, you will still gain benefit. The goal, no matter if you use one or all three of the techniques, is to place you in control. Whether you do so through your breath, with a visualization, with the way that you talk to yourself, or by using all three together, you can remove the distractions and silence the doubt—cut out that inner-critic altogether—and be prepared to move into action.

YOUR DAILY MVP

You want to be an MVP, don't you? Then you have to work for it, right? The most useful way to apply the previous chapter's MVP concept is to think about this as the daily process that prepares you to use BVT in the heat of performance. BVT is a process that can happen when managing the gaps during competition, those moments between races or bouts, the time in a huddle or when a teammate is shooting a free-throw. MVP is the practice you can work on that will make certain BVT will work when you need it. Think of MVP as training that occurs during practice for BVT that you'll use on competition day. MVP is brain-training you should work on every day of your life. These are mental reps, and you should look at training your mind no differently than training your body. You've got to do the work and you've got to do it with intention. If you're doing your daily MVP, you will become your most valuable player every day.

M **MEDITATION**

V **VISUALIZATION**

P **POSITIVE SELF-TALK**

If you want to be able to utilize WIN and activate BVT at a second's notice, you have to be devoted to the MVP process. It offers an elongated, developed approach developing good habits and applicable techniques that can transform your performances. It is MVP that develops mindfulness. Mindfulness creates clarity. You become more positive. With regular practice, you will have an overall better outlook, and as a result you will be able to navigate through the negativity surrounding you easier because your mind, body, and spirit are connected.

MEDITATE

Meditation starts with your breath, so you've already been exposed to a central component of meditative practice. Although here, rather than a rapid refocusing device to ground you in the moment, meditation builds off your controlled, sustained breathing as a practice to develop clarity and create calm. Even if you have never actively meditated before, you have likely encountered this applied awareness of breathing through participating in yoga, Qigong, or Tai Chi. Like so much of what we have discussed, meditation brings control and harnessing much of the untapped power of the mind. Meditation is a daily conditioning technique meant to align your mind, body, and spirit.

Meditation is one of those practices that is deceptively simple but that can take a lifetime to become good at performing. Many who have not attempted meditation hold false notions about it, including the belief that it is about emptying your mind, something that is virtually impossible. Rather than emptying the mind, meditation is all about creating a calm space in the mind, which in turn relaxes the body and creates clarity and room for intentionality. There are lots of formal practices and types of meditation taught, but they all share these basic premises aimed at forming interior quiet. Harnessing the power of achieving mental clarity is a foundational stone in maximizing your performance.

VISUALIZATION

Within BVT, visualization is a second step, though one that can be taken alone rapidly, in a systematic process for refocusing the mind and moving the body into the next action. In MVP, the parts of the process tend to be more blended. For example, one aspect of meditation can be to practice detailed visualizations. As much as you want to relax and have a clear mind during meditation, you can move in and out of the images that form your visualization as part of that meditation, so long as the images are all positive in their orientation. John Lester might visualize every pitch he would throw in a game, see and hear and feel those pitches in great detail, visualize himself executing each pitch with precision and perfect accuracy. Three-time Olympic gold medalist swimmer Ryan Murphy can, in meditation, visualize the entirety of a race, feel his power as he explodes from the wall on a start, see the speed of his flip at each turn, and sense the endurance present in his body as he accelerates in the closing segment.

You can help your ability to visualize by watching films of yourself performing at your best. Get out those game films and create a personal highlight reel. Carli Lloyd, a midfielder on the US Women's World Championship soccer team credits visualization with helping her prepare for the 2015 World Cup final. She is a regular practitioner of using MVP techniques because she realizes the value of building images of herself from specific past performances she wants to reproduce. While training just before the World Cup finals, Lloyd said she mentally visualized herself scoring four goals. While she didn't quite pull off four, she did score three—the first woman in World Cup history to do so.

There is a key physiological principle solidifying the importance of visualization for the athlete: the mind is largely incapable of distinguishing distinction between a physical action and an imagined one. While you cannot replace physical training and not lose ground, you *can* add visualization to your training regimen and gain ground. Research has revealed that mental practices are almost effective as true physical practices, and that doing both is more effective than doing either alone. Brain studies reveal that imagined actions (particularly richly detailed, intentional visualized actions) produce the same mental instructions for the brain as the actions themselves. This is true because mental imagery produces many cognitive processes in the brain: motor control, attention, perception, planning, and memory. So, the brain is being trained for actual performance during visualization.

For example, Guang Yue, an exercise psychologist from Cleveland Clinic Foundation in Ohio, researched the impacts of visualization with brain patterns in weightlifters and found that the patterns activated when a weightlifter worked out in the gym were similarly activated when they only imagined lifting. His study revealed that a cohort that lifted weights in a gym setting over a three-month period added thirty percent more muscle. Another cohort that only visualized similar weightlifting still gained 13.5 percent more muscle.[13] Because you are activating regions of the brain that parallel those used during activity, you literally are getting the physical benefit while also gaining confidence, experience, and a sense of control. This is why getting in your mental reps is so essential.

Champion golfer Jack Nicklaus famously said, "I never hit a shot, not even in practice, without having a very sharp, in-focus picture of it in my head. First, I see the ball where I want it to finish, nice and white and sitting up high on the bright green grass. Then the scene quickly changes, and I see the ball going there; its path, trajectory, and shape, even its behavior on landing." We can all learn to apply Nicklaus's use of visualization to our betterment.

POSITIVE SELF-TALK

When doing those daily mental MVPs, you should get in the habit of exiting the visualization by creating voiced positive, intentional affirmations. State your intentions. Find specific language that can give voice to your feelings and enhance your internal drive. Don't just say the words, see and feel them. Develop positivity and promote optimism with the language you employ. Find phrases that help you convey the joy you feel when at the heights of your competitive best or for the things for which you wish to show gratitude. These will

---

13   A.J. Adams, "Seeing Is Believing: The Power of Visualization," Psychology Today, December 3, 2009, https://www.psychologytoday.com/us/blog/flourish/200912/seeing-is-believing-the-power-visualization.

buoy you, raise you to your best self. Think about it; aren't we all our better selves when we live within the things in our lives for which we are grateful? That's a positive mindset that brings you energy. And energy is a product of achieving mindfulness, energy that can, in return, be channeled into our lives and our performances.

We need to tap into that positive energy when we're suddenly called into action, and building clear, repeated patterns of positive self-talk during your daily MVP practice can serve as a cue. There can be a direct connection between the affirmations we develop in MVP and those we employ as part of BVT.

Just as research has demonstrated the physiological benefits of visualization, psychological research has analyzed the benefits we gain from positive self-talk. From such research we can learn ways to find positivity, sustain it, and implement it in our practices. It's not enough for effective positive self-talk to say, "Okay, I'm a champion." To be effective, you have to feel the intention behind what you are doing, see yourself moving toward your goal, and feel forward momentum when you say positive phrases because they are going to lead to confidence and motivation. For many, developing the language you need and talking to yourself isn't enough, so consider the reinforcement and ownership that occurs when you begin to take that self-talk and write it down or you put it in a recording, and you share that self-talk, and the intention behind it, with your teammates and your coaches.

When I work with clients, I always start with the affirmation statements "I am, I can, and I will."

Often, I'll tell them, "Before you start your game, I want you to write five things that say 'I am _____. These might be, "I am confident or I am a champion." Then I tell them to write five statements that say "I will _____. I will be confident, I will communicate." Then we talk through these inventories. From these discussions, together we form the basis for applying specific words for specific situations.

We also need to understand the language that we shouldn't speak, words that don't serve us as competitors. Words like "hope." You may find this strange, seeing "hope" as a positive affirmation, but I hear the word and it's like a needle scratching a favorite, unblemished vinyl record because

HOPE IS NOT A STRATEGY.

"hope" is speculative, it leaves room for doubt. "I hope I do well today," is not radically different from "I think I'll do well today" or "I might do well today." I want performers to say "I am going to do well today." Hope is not a strategy. When you are only thinking you're going to do something, you're standing still.

BRINGING IT ALL TOGETHER

You already know how to get better by dedicating time to training your body, developing your skills, and building your knowledge. You do so every day in practice and at the gym. You do it every day on the job, working after hours, skipping vacation days when the job demands. And you already work to grow the intellectual side of your brain in the way you spend time in the film room and studying the playbook, just as you do by reading, taking courses, gaining certifications, and attending conferences. So why don't you train the other needs of the mind with as much diligence, those that generate confidence, qualm fear, and spark joy? All you need to accomplish this training is already within you. Allow yourself to become the master of your own techniques. Choose the positive affirmations and the images that are most comfortable for you and whatever provides you the most value. Doing so will help you develop the qualities of mental toughness the next three chapters will develop in sequence: resilience, tenacity, and grit.

Developing a WIN mindset, creating and following BVT when in the midst of the action, and preparing yourself for achieving excellence by the daily practice of MVP will set you apart from your competitors and help you realize the most of your abilities.

CHAPTER 5

BEND LIKE BAMBOO

Training the Subconscious Mind

The Bamboo that bends is stronger than the oak that resists.

—Zen Proverb

We have all experienced getting in the car while distracted by something that's troubling us and then surprising ourselves to find that we arrived safely home with no memory of driving. We can get home because we've already learned the way and the body can perform when it is called upon.

To train for the unknown or the unexpected, we must develop the mental toughness to endure hours of training the mind and body in order to wire the subconscious mind to be prepared at a moment's notice. The subconscious mind allows us to react in moments without thought because the mind and body have experienced certain movements, acts, and tasks many times over; subconsciously the mind will direct the body in the right direction, just like that car trip home.

We can accomplish such things because of unique properties that are built into how the human brain interprets incoming information and how it interacts with the body and with familiar environments. For more than a century, scientists have recognized the existence of "automatism" or implicit procedural memories that allow us to perform complicated actions without conscious thought. Automatic skills based on implicit learning include most common daily skills we master through practice, practice, practice. Much of this ability flows through us as a fusion of emotion and information, an amalgam of physiological processes and electrical impulses. This chapter will examine both the more mystical, metaphysical aspects of mental resiliency and the physiology of the human brain. Many of the ideas I turn to have their roots in the practices that form foundations of Buddhist thought and have entered Western experience through things like the practice of yoga. But we'll also turn to the science that backs the validity of these practices, including a little bit of exploration of brain biochemistry through phenomena such as how neural pathways are formed.

PURSUE RESILIENCY

The most important quality that runs through all of this chapter is the idea of resiliency, which is why the epigraph for the chapter means so much to me: I believe that in order to "bend it like Beckham," you've got to learn to bend like bamboo. Bamboo has a lot of qualities that we can see as metaphor and apply to our lives and our approach to performance. Perhaps the most familiar and most important quality of bamboo is its strength, strength that comes mostly through its flexibility. As the proverb suggests, a mighty wind can break an oak tree, considered among the hardest wood of the forest, but the bamboo survives because it bends with the wind. It is flexible, yet its roots are firmly planted in the soil so it has a sturdy foundation. I always picture a forest after a heavy snow. A sudden, wet storm can stack up on branches and break them, but the bamboo flexes, bending with the weight of the snow, then springs back upright, shrugging off the weight.

We must learn to apply bamboo's flexibility and bend with resiliency when we face difficult challenges rather than stiffen up. It's the springing back that matters. Just as our bodies must be flexible, so must our minds. We have to face the truth of the adage, "What you resist persists." If instead you breathe into difficult challenges and you bend, then you flow with the situation you face. You become adaptable and you trust the MVP work you have done. Your body will respond when you call on it. When the emotional hurricane hits full force and we're surrounded by chaos; time is running out on the game clock; your opponent has hit you with something totally unexpected; you're hurt or you've lost an important teammate for the remainder of the game—that's when we need to trust ourselves the most, breathe, and draw on the power of our mental training. Our brains are powerful beyond belief, and we, in our subconscious mind, constantly hunger to learn.

Tapping into the power of your subconscious mind means applying all the processes we discussed in the last chapter. They provide the training ground for the mind. The roots for those processes go back to ancient practices. For example, in the chanting that sometimes accompanies traditional yoga, we not only find the rhythm to guide our breathing, we have mantras that parallel the positive self-talk we also find in modern psychology. That self-talk quickly channels intention into action; it's there to call upon because we've practiced it. We've trained the body to associate the positive energy the mind has developed through focus on the meaning behind our intention. When we train the mind and the body together, they work as they are meant to, as one coordinated mechanism. You might not be able to fathom the speed at which your brain processes the complex commands to take a physical action—spring into the air, twist to the right, extend your left arm, track the ball with your eyes, listen for your opponent's breath as he/she tries to out-jump you, push him/her off with your other arm, close the fingers of the left hand. But you can train the mind to know that we are capable of that extra half-inch of vertical leap, to know that you've worked so repeatedly to catch the ball with one hand it will respond when called upon, to see your opponent's eyes with such intensity of focus as you collide that you react instantly and ask your body to choose an angle that provides you control. This is the point where self-talk has cemented belief, confidence, and focus, and finalized the link between the need for self-belief and the call to action.

THE IMPRESSIVE, TRANSFORMATIVE BRAIN

All I describe is possible because, just as you can build muscle, the brain responds to "mental workouts." Every day we are changing our brains because we are learning new things, calling up old memories, and encountering new environments. Studying the brain's ability to learn and adapt was one of the most fascinating parts of my master's degree coursework and I remain fascinated with the science behind these abilities found in the literature of my discipline. This transformative ability of the brain is called **neural plasticity**. Our neural pathways enable a signal to be sent from one part of the nervous system to another through synapses. They form an electrical circuit capable of transmitting information, and as we learn new things, the synapses that form the connections are strengthened. This means that every time you remember something, the neural path to that memory is strengthened. Brain plasticity appears to be the physiological basis for the possibility of transforming our minds. What's more, the brain subconsciously creates neuromuscular patterns similar to those constructed during physical movement. With increasingly sophisticated brain imaging techniques, we can see what the brain is capable of at the highest level of physical and mental expertise.

By mobilizing our thoughts and practicing new ways of thinking, we can reshape our nerve cells and change the way our brains work. And just like a hiking trail, the most worn path is the strongest and easiest to travel. So, a good way to think about it is: "Stuff sticks where you sit." If you focus on stress with your thoughts and feelings, you strengthen stress pathways. By contrast, if you focus on calmness with your thoughts and feelings, you strengthen

IF YOU HAVE A DEEP-ROOTED NEGATIVE BELIEF SYSTEM AND YOU FAIL TO ADDRESS IT, YOU'VE LITERALLY SET YOURSELF UP FOR A SELF-FULFILLING PROPHECY.

relaxation pathways. Sometimes we must, figuratively speaking, clear the brush, form the scattered rocks into steps, and shore up the low spots to build the trail of a new neural pathway. If you have a deep-rooted negative belief system and you fail to address it, you've literally set yourself up for a self-fulfilling prophecy. But we can rewire brain circuits if we'll put in the practice.

For the needs of the next one up mindset, this alignment between intentional practice and literal transformation can happen in large part because of something we have explored earlier: the brain doesn't really differentiate between the detailed imagining of a thing and the actual doing of it. The information of the imagined image is processed in a similar manner to information learned by physical actions. There is a close relationship between body experience and memory. Our brain constantly creates the experience of one's own body in space by combining information from multiple senses: sight, hearing, touch. So, when a tennis player like Serena Williams visualizes a serve, the electrical activity in her brain mimics the same activity in her brain when she is serving the ball. This is why your mental reps are every bit as important as your physical ones and why you want to make certain you are doing the "right" reps—those that create focus, concentration, positivity, calmness, and joy. Mental reps need to mirror your other training reps in terms of using proper technique. Your form needs to be right, just like you pay attention to the right positioning of your body when you're lifting weights.

There are a lot of additional benefits from focusing on mind/body alignment. This connection is a two-way street. Several studies have shown that high-level athletes often have superior physical abilities, such as faster reaction times or better visual acuity. This is likely true because they are constantly in environments where such traits are needed. Studies have also shown that highly competitive athletes are extremely skilled at anticipating their opponent's movement. They do so because they pay constant and close attention to the smallest details of their opponent's physical stance, body language, and nonverbal cues.

But activating such abilities can flow the other way as well, and you can train mentally to assist in the physical needs you have.

For example, Michelle Voss, a psychologist, reported on studies that monitor athletes' abilities at changing the breadth of visual attention—the ability to focus on what is currently relevant to whatever you are doing while ignoring distractions. You can train your brain to expand how many things and how much of the environment you can pay attention to at one time. Voss explains:

> For example, a wide breadth of attention is necessary for driving in a busy roadway where there are cross-walks with bold pedestrians jumping out at any moment compounded with bike lanes, merging traffic, potential stoplights, and maybe even your GPS companion directing you where to go. Think downtown Chicago at rush-hour. Now imagine you find yourself lost and while at a stoplight you decide to really "focus" on the map on your GPS module. You tune out the radio, any yapping passengers, all street sounds and sights, and direct tunnel vision to the GPS screen.[14]

This heightened focus is something we are chasing during athletic performance; your brain contains all the tools necessary to develop that focus. Think of it as if you carry a lab within you that can make the exact pair of glasses you need to see with clarity.

FLEXIBILITY, VULNERABILITY, AND HUMILITY

Bamboo can be deceptive, as it looks weak. And if you cut it open, it is hollow, which ultimately is part of its beauty, for it achieves real strength with grace. This is a lesson for all of us in several ways as

---

14   Michelle Voss, "Understanding the Mind of the Elite Athlete," *Scientific American,* June 1, 2010, https://www.scientificamerican.com/article/understanding-elite-athlete/.

well.

To truly be capable of the kind of mental flexibility and resiliency and bend when a situation calls for it, you must be willing to be vulnerable. What I mean by vulnerability is a willingness to show up, step in with both feet, get really grounded, and trust your subconscious. At the heart of that process is the MVP.

When I work with someone, whether an athlete or a corporate athlete who lacks self-confidence, I can't really help them change that trait unless they are willing to be vulnerable as well. Because usually what I find is that there is some deeply rooted issue that has created the negativity they suffer from. To address it, they have to be willing to open up, talk it through, and be committed to enough self-exploration to identify to face their fear. What you will eventually find is that, like bamboo, being willing to confront these feelings of weakness is exactly what will make you strong.

From a coaching perspective, helping people tap into the deeper parts of themselves takes the careful establishment of trust. Once they open up and face the roots of their fear, then they can develop the processes we have been talking about that will provide them the means to transform their subconscious mind. This is a big part of what the next one up mindset is all about, because it is that time you spend preparing for your opportunity when you can build the processes and the self-belief needed to allow you to seize the day when it arrives.

And once that day does arrive, how will you manage your success? I'd argue that if we let it go to our heads, if we go beyond celebrating success (something we all should do) and instead become braggarts, we end up killing the very forces, energies, and processes that got us there. In my experience, the most gifted, most successful people tend to be quite humble. They are confident in themselves, so much so they don't have to talk about their accomplishments. I think humility takes a lot of courage. When you can achieve the humble mindset, it leaves you space to focus on the right things and not get caught up in distractions. We can learn to be humble when we respect the power of transformation of which we are capable, respect the power of our minds, and recognize the difference between the quiet focus and potency we can develop from mindfulness and the energized confidence we will need to draw from it when we enter the arena of competition. Then we can become the fullest equivalent of the Samurai—the calm, prepared, balanced mind that can release its fearsome warrior at any moment.

ENTERING THE ZONE

Perhaps the pinnacle of activated mindfulness is the experience of what is popularly referred to as achieving "flow" or being in the "zone." I use the two words interchangeably though personally prefer the phrase "locked in." Most people may not ever truly experience this feeling. I'm fortunate that I have several times. Everyone's memory of being "locked in" is different. For some, the action around them moves really fast; for others, events seem to happen in slow motion. Sounds can be really loud or deathly quiet. In my own experience, things are bright: vivid and clear. I get tunnel vision, with things in the periphery becoming foggy. I am not fully aware of my own actions; they just seem to arrive as the most natural motions I can imagine. It is a blissful thing when it happens, and I do believe it can be a result of all the processes this book focuses on, but I don't think it is something athletes should necessarily be chasing. It's more important to create the habits that might lead to it and cultivate the environment where your mind and body may integrate into that perfect kind of harmony. Be steadfast in your processes, train your mind, bend with the pressure and you're far more likely to experience this phenomenon. If you don't, don't stress over it, you will still have entered a state of consciousness that allows you to do what you need to do. Like everything else we have discussed, it's more important that you stick to controlling the things you can control. If the gift of experiencing being locked in comes along, consider it a special moment that you have earned and stick to the work that got you there.

CHAPTER 6

SHIELDS ARE OPTIONAL

Releasing Your Inner Warrior

*I don't run away from a challenge because I am
afraid. Instead, I run toward it because the only way
to escape fear is to trample it beneath your feet.*

—*Nadia Comăneci, five-time Olympic gold medalist, gymnastics*

Y ou've likely seen the Maori Haka dance performed live, on television, or in a YouTube video—that bug-eyed, wide-stanced stomping ritual filled with tongues protruding, palms slapping thighs, fists slamming biceps accompanied by a loudly chanted song. Whether you've seen actual Maori warriors reenacting the battlefield intimidation tactics or the infamous All Blacks stomping together in formation prior to a rugby match, once you've seen it, you won't forget it. And as odd of a display as it may have seemed, you'd be intimidated if you were their opponent.

I first encountered the Haka dance when it was performed by a group of football players at Junípero Serra High School in San Mateo, a team that had a number of players hailing from island nations of the Pacific, though the whole team had embraced the Haka. I thought it was the coolest, most motivating thing I'd ever seen.

Whether we embrace intimidation as part of our game or not, we're all competitors. We will all be asked to place ourselves in impossible situations. And we'll all be required to dig deep within and prove that we are up to the task.

SPORT DEMANDS THAT WE BE MENTALLY TOUGH. IT IS THE NEED FOR TENACITY THAT IS AT OUR WARRIOR HEARTS WHEN IT COMES TO ATHLETIC COMPETITION AND COMPETITIVE BUSINESS NEEDS.

Athletic competition, and some high-stakes elements of competitive corporate life, not only bears a great deal of resemblance to warfare—close groups of like-minded individuals competing against rivals, with uniforms, pageantry, extreme physical exertion—it also asks us to call upon our warrior spirits. Many sports can trace their evolution directly from warfare, whether that's as overt as the javelin or more in the vein of the organized brutality of rugby. Sport demands that we be mentally tough. It is the need for tenacity that is at our warrior hearts when it comes to athletic competition and competitive business needs. In his book *Kodo: Ancient Ways*, Kensho Furuya reminds us of the link between this tenacious need and the resiliency we discussed in the last chapter: "The warrior, like bamboo, is ever ready for action."[15]

Think about the quarterback in football. How often is he placed in a game circumstance where, in order to complete the play, by the very nature of its design he knows he must wait for his receiver to get open; inevitably that also means knowing he will get hit by a defensive end the size of a Buick charging at full speed. To stay in the pocket and complete the throw when every bit of common sense and bodily instinct tells him to run away defines the tenacity of mental toughness.

If you're a warrior—I don't care if you're a soldier, if you're an athlete, or if you're in the corporate environment—you want to be the best version of yourself. You must find the inner-resolve to battle through difficulty. You must compete when you're exhausted or hurt or trying to stand tall against what appears on paper to be a superior opponent. To be successful, the roots of such warrior ability are in properly using your BVT and your MVP. And traditionally, dating all the way back to the ancient Samurai, warriors have knowingly used all three aspects of MVP. For Samurai, training tirelessly and visualizing the worst that could happen gave them a feeling of control while in battle. Maintaining control, particularly of one's own mind, is at the heart of the way of the Samurai. In a modern warrior application of Samurai principles, the US Navy dramatically increased SEAL passing rates by teaching recruits psychological methods for gaining a feeling of control.[16] The Samurai Kaibara Ekken (1630 – 1714) said: "A noble man controls frivolity with gravity, awaits action in a state of calm. It is important for the spirit to be whole, the mood steady, and the mind unmoving."

---

15 Kensho Furuya, *Ancient Ways* (Black Belt Communications, 1996).

16 "The 4 Psychological Techniques That Increased Navy SEAL Passing Rates," Barking Up The Wrong Tree, accessed March 4, 2019, https://www.bakadesuyo.com/2009/11/how-the-navy-seals-increased-passing-rates/.

WHAT DOES YOUR WARRIOR LOOK LIKE?

This is a question I ask all my clients. I ask it because they will have to regularly call upon the strongest parts of themselves to be the performers they need to be. For some, this literally means creating a kind of alter ego so that they can turn on their performance when in competition and turn it off when they return to civilian life. Being able to see or name your warrior can provide a way to channel those parts of yourself you need when in the heat of competition.

Perhaps one of the most famous warrior transformations is that of the legendary Kobe Bryant, who saw himself as consciously developing an entire alter ego. In an interview on *The Hollywood Reporter's Award Chatter* podcast, Bryant explained why he felt this need, which came at a time when he was facing knee surgery and dealing with the backlash and legal issues stemming from a sexual assault charge filed in Colorado in 2003. He told the interviewer, "It just felt like the game, which was always like a safe haven for me, was being compromised, as well. I needed to create some sort of an alter ego, just for myself, so when I step out on the court, I'm somebody different, not the person that was sitting in a courthouse … and it helped me for my sanity. And then it just turned into something more."[17] The something more became "The Black Mamba" and embracing this deadly predator allowed him to differentiate the troubles of his personal life from his need to perform.

I encountered another rich example of the power of a transformational vision of oneself at a high school where I was working with the football team. We had one player who wore Superman socks

---

17   Tariq Saleh, "Kobe Bryant explains meaning behind famous 'Black Mamba' nickname," Gamesport, accessed March 4, 2019, https://www.givemesport. com/1163752-kobe-bryant-explains-meaning-behind-famous-black-mamba-nickname.

rather than the regular team socks, and he wore a Superman t-shirt underneath his pads. He told me that as soon as he put his pads over his shirt, he felt like he had transformed, just like Clark Kent in the phone booth. He was no longer the guy who had walked into the locker room, he was Superman. And he played like Superman. He morphed from this easy-going, likeable, nondescript high school kid to a superhero. You saw it in how he carried himself, how he played, how he interacted with his teammates. That's the thing about a warrior mindset, it's like letting go of the civilian—the student athlete, the boyfriend, the son or daughter, the father or mother—and turning into something else that is powerful and prepared and supremely confident.

I've seen a similar transformation in one of my clients Aja Evans, an Olympic bronze medalist, member of the US National Bobsled Team, and former track and field athlete. Aja is quiet, polite, well-spoken, yet in the heat of competition she becomes an outspoken force to be reckoned with, more than capable of holding her own, against her brother, an NFL defensive tackle. Facing the bobsled track, her game face comes out and you see her warrior spirit.

SUPREME CONFIDENCE

Both my mentor Graham Betchart and I define supreme confidence as confidence that extends beyond the moment. When you are confident in your process, confident in your body, and confident in your thoughts, you develop a lasting confidence that can carry you beyond mistakes. When you are supremely confident, it won't matter if you miss five shots in a row or if you drop the pass that would have been a game-winner, because you have become a person capable of rebounding beyond the mistake or the poor performance. This sort of elemental confidence is key to the warrior mentality, because the very nature of sport, which pushes the human to attempt perfection, is constantly filled with mistakes. Errors are an inevitability of high-level athletic performance because of the intricacy of the competition, the single-mindedness of your opponent, and the limitations of the body. Show me a SLS Super Crown World Champion skateboarder who has never fallen while trying to master a trick. This is one of the reasons athletics is such good preparation for life, because who hasn't made mistakes on the job? The supreme confidence of a properly trained mind is central to developing real grit, which we discuss at more length in the next chapter.

In order to become a resilient person, the warrior mindset must exist in preparation, as well as in performance. Among the teams I have worked with are women's and men's programs at Archbishop Mitty High School in San Jose, where the teams are frequently ranked nationally, and the academic expectations are equally demanding. Like high school athletes anywhere, students have to deal with homework, exams, college applications, scholarship essays, peer pressure, romantic relationships, coaches and administrators, their parents, and hormones. That's a lot of pressure that's only multiplied by being on an elite-level team. Grow that kind of pressure a thousand-fold when you think of professional and Olympic athletes who add to that list the pressures of media scrutiny, endorsements, sponsorships, contracts, and every sort of leach and huckster trying to claim a part of their fame and fortune. How do they leave all the distraction

IN ORDER TO BECOME A RESILIENT PERSON, THE WARRIOR MINDSET MUST EXIST IN PREPARATION, AS WELL AS IN PERFORMANCE.

behind when they step onto the hardwood of the practice court or the turf of the training field and be completely 100 percent immersed into getting 1 percent better that day as an athlete?

One need is to have a cue, something that shifts you out of your civilian clothes the way that high school player did when he placed his pads atop his Superman t-shirt. For me, it was as simple as putting on a towel that draped from the front of my pants where I could wipe my hands; once it was in place, I was ready to go. My friends said they could see my transformation in the way I ran out of the locker room, could sense that something inside of me had shifted into warrior mode.

Cues are different for everyone. They are a mechanism for entering the mental space needed to excel. I work with a seventy-year-old fencer and her warrior mindset is a tiger. At the Summer Nationals she took me by surprise when she pulled down her vest and revealed a tiger tattoo that went all the way up her arm and onto the top of her chest. She laughed at my shocked response and then admitted it was only a temporary tattoo, but she said, "I've got my inner tiger with me in this competition. I'm ready to go."

We don't need to get tattoos, real or fake, to develop the cues we need to embrace our warrior selves, but we can consciously create scenarios and develop mind/body connections that help us enter this confident, competitive mindset. What we are asking from ourselves and the processes we employ is a mindfulness that lets us embrace the best parts of ourselves and provides us energy. Amy Cuddy, social psychologist and author of *Presence*, explains part of what led her to a question that explores such a connection in the phenomenon she labels "power posing":

As scientists, the first thing we needed was a clear hypothesis. This was our thinking: if nonverbal expressions of power are so hardwired that we instinctively throw our arms up in a V when we win a race—regardless of cultural background, gender, or whether we've seen anyone else do it—and if William James was right that our emotions are as much a result as they are a cause of our physical expressions, then what would happen if we adopt expansive postures even when we are feeling powerless? Since we naturally expand our bodies when we feel powerful, do we also naturally feel powerful when we expand our bodies?[18]

By altering your presence with your body, you can gain confidence and move into a state of mental toughness. Cuddy essentially asks, what if, before you depart for an interview, you throw your hands up in a victory stance as if you have just won an event and see yourself saying, "Yes!"? Feeling the emotion you get in victory, tapping into your own presence, transforms into the body language you use, how you carry yourself, how you feel about yourself, and it creates the confidence and toughness you need to nail that interview.

I have experienced the phenomena Cuddy talks about many times when working with clients, including the opposite of such presence. One such experience stands out in my mind. I once worked with a high school football free safety who possessed a tremendously athletic physique and a great mind, but he lacked an edge that allowed him to play up to his potential. He was going into his senior year, but had spent all his time on Junior Varsity. He was a physical specimen, 6'2", at the prime of his physical life, and he was smart, a player who asked a lot of questions, was engaged, and liked directing the defense. All his coaches thought, "This guy's going to rock it" as he emerged from summer practices, and yet in the first scrimmage

---

18   Amy Cuddy, *Presence* (New York: Little Brown and Company, 2015).

he produced mediocre play. Then, during the first game, he melted down; by the second game, his fear was evident. His coaches pulled him out after the first quarter of the third game because they could see he was literally about to cry.

I started working with him the next week. I really wanted to figure out what was going on inside his mind. I asked him, "What do you like about hitting someone?"

"I like to stop them," he said.

I clarified what I was asking. I told him, "When people play safety, they'll say stuff like, 'I love taking someone's head off, I like shutting someone down, I like putting them in the ground.' Do you feel that?"

He looked at me, and said, "No." When I pressed him about why he thought he didn't, he explained, "Because everybody wants me to be like what you're saying, I just want to be who I am out of football. I don't want to change who I am on the football field."

"Well, why not?"

"Because that's not me."

I asked him, "So why do you play football?"

"Because all my friends are playing." The whole time we talked, this muscular, fit young man sat in the locker room, hunched over, his body turned into itself, closed and protective in its posture.

I looked at him and I said, "Feel your posture right now." Then I told him, "Just do me a favor and sit straight up." And as soon as he sat straight up and put his shoulders back, his whole face changed and opened into a smile. "Does that feel better?" I asked. Then I explained, "What's happening is that your subconscious mind is so heavy with emotion and worrying about other people's perspectives, you play scared. Why don't you walk in this world differently? Because you can. You can actually change your warrior mindset if you want to." Finally, I asked him, "Doesn't it feel good to see life up here instead of down there?"

That young man was a prime example of someone who didn't have a warrior mindset. More than that, he was an example of a player who gave in to fear. Football might not have been his thing, which is fine, and it's important that we are honest with ourselves about our motivations and our intentions, but the lesson of finding confidence, alongside the lesson of allowing yourself to feel happiness, is a universal one that young man can carry into all aspects of his life. He'll find battles, the same as the rest of us.

EMBRACE FEAR

What we must do is find the tools, techniques, and processes to face those battles headlong. Price Pritchett, an author best known for books on leadership, reminds us, "People seldom get in touch with their deepest strengths and greatest abilities until it's forced upon them by major challenges. Only then do we really have the opportunity to discover ourselves and the world of possibilities." Garett Tujague, the offensive line coach for the Virginia Cavaliers football team talks about our need to embrace the struggle. He said when I interviewed him for my podcast, "If you don't push yourself to the brink, how are you going to know what you are capable of?" His teams practice hard and play hard. When they take the field, they charge, their arms linked like warriors entering combat. He echoes the winningest skier in World Cup history, Lindsey Vonn,

> **"IF YOU DON'T PUSH YOURSELF TO THE BRINK, HOW ARE YOU GOING TO KNOW WHAT YOU ARE CAPABLE OF?"**

who has said that fear is the last thing on her mind. "I don't really get afraid. I kind of feel like fear is kind of a pointless emotion, because if you're afraid, you're never going to accomplish the things you want to accomplish."[19]

Of course, the consequences of not embracing your inner warrior can be great. Unchecked fear leads into anxiety, which can have significant mental health consequences. Tujague reminds us, "Fear lives in the future, guilt lives in the past." This is precisely why we must adopt the WIN mindset and live only in the moment, as the warrior does.

A good starting point for embracing fear is to ask, "Is there such a thing as good fear?" Of course, there is. We've all used the expression "healthy fear." This suggests there is a way of rationalizing fear, which is important for the kind of fear we face in performance is fear of our own making. I introduced the acronym I like for FEAR earlier: False Evidence Appearing Real. If we can accept that we are the ones responsible for creating our own fear, then we can begin to have a relationship with it. If you have no relationship with it, then the fear controls you. Once we accept that we have created the fear, that it is a product of our mind, then we can control it and remove it from our lives. When fear arises, there's no room for procrastination, we must run right at it.

I once saw this little gem on a bumper sticker. It's well worth keeping in mind. "There's no sense being pessimistic. It wouldn't work anyway."

When we see that opponent who enters the competition with swagger, when you can feel the confidence radiating off of them and

---

19   "Lindsey Vonn: Fear Is a Pointless Emotion," Mid-day.com, last
        modified January 20, 2018, https://www.mid-day.com/articles/
        lindsey-vonn-fear-is-a-pointless-emotion/18956169.

you begin to think, "Oh my God, they're the defending champion, no one can match up with them," instead of giving into the anxiety that comes with seeing their power, we must instead combat it with the realization that this is exactly the circumstance we've trained for: we're experienced over years of performance; we must respond with "Let's go do this!" Start thinking about your assets and solutions vs. negative thoughts and emotions. These are the moments where we have to draw on our inner warrior. We can't control the opponent, so we must control ourselves. Remember what the Samurai taught us, great warriors are disciplined.

"I often refer to our players as elite warriors, not because they are going to war and certainly not because what we are doing is anything as serious as war, but because they are trained in an incredibly rigorous way and are constantly engaged in physical, mental, and spiritual combat."

— URBAN MEYER

Football Coach, Ohio State University, University of Florida, University of Utah

---

CHAPTER 7

WHEN YOUR EIGHTY-FIVE-YEAR-OLD HIP FAILS YOUR THIRTY-YEAR-OLD BODY

Applying Grit for Overcoming Injury and Adversity

When you fall, get right back up.

—*Lindsey Vonn, Olympic gold medalist and winner
of seventy-eight World Cups, downhill skiing*

When I was playing quarterback at Chabot Junior College, I suffered a compressed fracture of my left hip. This was the root of the debilitating injury I introduced in the prologue. At the time, it was an injury that nagged me, but it didn't stop me. I warriored on. After my junior year playing at Sonoma State University, I realized my body was breaking down. My hip clicked whenever I moved and caused me pain. I also had to get a cortisone shot in my shoulder just to finish my season. With the pain I was in I knew I couldn't take my game to the next level, so I ended up moving away from football altogether. And when I left the game I started to move away from my identity as well, because being an athlete was all I'd known. That hip injury ended up shaping nearly everything in my life for almost two decades.

As a quarterback, I'd spent my athletic career as a leader. And I'd been quite successful, breaking records and wrapping much of my self-esteem in my ability. The more my hip hurt, the more the qualities that had made me a successful leader faded. Ten years removed from the game, I had developed a pronounced limp, so pronounced that my shoes showed unnatural wear patterns in the heels.

I HAD LOST THE FIGHT OF BEING A WARRIOR.

Because I was in constant pain, I self-medicated by drinking and using marijuana. I was overweight and unhappy. I no longer participated in team activities, even for recreation. Doctors told me, "You're too young to get a hip replacement."

I had lost the fight of being a warrior.

At thirty-six, I consulted with one of the doctors for the Oakland A's. I told him about the pain I was in, including the fact that I was losing sleep. That was the ticket. It made the difference for him to recommend hip replacement. And I thought, "That's it? I should have told you that ten years ago."

The surgery went well, although in the recovery room the surgeon told me, "Your hip looks like it belongs to an eighty-five-year-old man and you had the four biggest bone spurs I've ever removed from the human body." Usually a hip replacement takes about an hour and a half. Mine took three and a half hours. The doctor went through two sets of scrubs.

Although the surgery went fine, my body did not react well to the trauma it had been put through. Thirty days after the surgery they took the first post-operative x-ray and saw a growth on my hip. The doctor said, "What is that?" I replied, "You tell me, you're the doctor." Uncertain what he was seeing, the doctor determined that they needed to monitor my condition closely and requested that I return every thirty days.

Every month that spot on the x-ray grew bigger and bigger. The doctor determined it was a condition called heterotopic ossification. When we suffer any kind of wound, our brain sends a message to rally the body to heal it. My body, apparently, went into overdrive. The rate of acceleration of scar tissue my body produced was extremely rare. It was of the sort most often found in soldiers who had lost limbs in combat. On top of my hip flexor, which allows our hips to move back and forth and side to side, there was a bone that grew six inches long and four inches wide.

I had entered the surgery thinking I was going to have a new life again, that I could put all the pain and the identity crisis behind me. Instead the doctors told me, "We've got to sit this out as long as possible and make sure this bone fully grows. How long that is going to take? We don't know."

A year later, the alteration to the way I walked was ten times worse than before and the pain was constant. Each year that passed, the pain and body transformation became more debilitating. Because of the alteration to my posture and my stride as my body tried to compensate for this unnatural six-inch bone, my spine twisted in three spots. My hands would go numb when I slept. I couldn't clip my toenails or tie my shoes for over three years. I couldn't use a public restroom without my leg sticking into the adjacent stall.

All I wanted was to be normal.

Eventually the doctor told me, "You have to be okay with being handicapped," before handing me a placard for parking in designated spaces. I had hung on for three years when the doctor called and told me he had consulted with colleague in Europe who recommended they remove the scar tissue and then treat the area with intensity-modulated radiation therapy (IMRT) to hope it would prevent the bone from growing back. My doctor gave me six months to prepare myself for the surgery.

I wanted to enter this surgery with an entirely different mindset than I had with the hip replacement. I wanted my body as ready as it could be, and I set about losing weight and working out in any way my body could accommodate the bone spur. Equally importantly, I set about getting my mind ready—spiritually and emotionally—I wanted to enter with a positive belief system and get out of the funk I'd been in for years. I wanted to seize this opportunity to change my life.

The moment I got out of that surgery and the bone had been removed, it felt like I awoke to a world where everything was vibrant and clear. When the recovery room personnel asked me, "Hey, Mr. Parr, how are you doing?" I answered "I'm back!" And that was exactly how it felt, like the old me had returned.

Within two weeks of the surgery, even as my doctor and physical therapist were telling me I needed to wait six to twelve weeks before I started really putting stress on the hip, my response was "Screw this. I've been waiting almost two decades." I began working out and my body responded well. I felt like I was a warrior again. I had reawakened my inner athlete.

I share my story simply because I've been there. I have faced real adversity. If anything, the two decades it took for me to heal and to find my inner warrior again only makes me more aware of the need to get your mind right in order to stand up to difficulty. Healing the body won't be enough when you battle to return from serious injury, and it will require a mind/body meld if we are to develop the mental toughness required to face the inevitable adversity we will encounter. My ultimate post-recovery realization was that I deserved happiness. And, building upon that realization, I began to form the steps of a plan that would eventually lead me away from a high-paying but low-satisfaction corporate job where I'd been very successful, and into the education and hard work of starting my own business and building the knowledge that has allowed me to write the book you now hold in your hands.

TRANSFORMING WITH GRIT

The third element of mental toughness linked with resiliency and tenacity is grit. I define grit as that thing within you that will not allow you to quit. This is the part of mental toughness that we associate with people like Navy SEALs, those who say that it doesn't matter what you throw at me, I'm never going to give up. I went too many years without really displaying the grit that I needed. But, over the long haul, I learned to discover it again.

Garret Tujague has a picture in his office at the University of Virginia of a stork eating a frog; the frog is firmly in the stork's beak and the frog is holding onto the outside of the beak for dear life. Both refuse to let go. One or the other is going to die in the battle. For Tujague, this battle of wills to outlast the other epitomizes grit.

Stronger even than that image and making the story of my own injury pale by comparison, is Bella Picard. As a sophomore, the standout hitter, notorious speedster, and starting center fielder for St. Joseph's University softball team was playing in a game against Fordham when her coaches signaled for a hit and run with Bella on first. She already had ten stolen bases that season, and Bella was known as a fearless player willing to sacrifice her body to help her team. When her teammate swung and missed, Bella went for the steal. True to her warrior spirit, seeing the throw coming in from the catcher, Bella executed a head-first slide into second, only she slammed into the knees of the Fordham shortstop stepping into the baseline to make the catch. Bella was knocked unconscious and lay motionless. Once she came to, she was aware that her neck hurt and that she had a tingling sensation in her right arm.

Writer Storms Reback explains the outcome of that collision:

> She was taken to the emergency room at Lincoln Medical Center, where doctors told her she'd broken her C5 vertebra. Over the course of the next few days the tingling sensation in her arm grew more intense and spread down her right leg. After being transferred to New York Presbyterian Hospital, Picard awoke three days after the accident to discover she couldn't move the entire right side of her body.[20]

Bella underwent spinal fusion surgery and regained some sensation in the pinky finger of her right hand, but the doctors informed her that, best-case scenario, it would still take two to three years before she was walking again.

Bella immediately made it clear that her goal wasn't just to regain the use of her right side, but to play softball again. She insisted on an aggressive therapy schedule, pushing her body to its limit. Six months later, after a daily grind of neuromuscular re-education and relentless physical therapy, Bella shocked everyone when she took a

---

20 Storms Reback, "The Relentless Spirit of Bella Picard," FloSoftball, May 31, 2017, https://www.flosoftball.com/articles/5066042-the-relentless-spirit-of-bella-picard.

few steps on her own. Over time, she has had to relearn all the skills she once took for granted. Reback tells of her gritty determination:

> When she lived in the rehab hospital, she slept with a softball in her bed and at the end of each therapy session she would practice simply trying to hold it in her right hand. By the end of that summer, she could grip a softball with the pinky and ring finger of her right hand and fling the ball in a catapult-like motion. "I said to myself, 'I will be throwing a softball next spring,' and I did it," Bella said.[21]

She continued to set other goals: to play softball again, to hold the children she wanted one day in the future, to remove the leg brace that aids her ability to walk, even if that moment didn't arrive until she was on her death bed. According to Reback, part of Bella's life ethic that keeps her accomplishing each of the goals she creates for herself is found when she says, "It keeps you emotionally healthy to have faith in yourself. You're not bound to your situation. You always have a choice."[22] Bella Picard has defied every prediction her doctors made, and while she has not returned to college softball, she can dive and catch and throw with an ability few can duplicate. If you ever wish to be inspired, simply search YouTube for videos of her. She epitomizes grit, never once giving up on her recovery. I've had the pleasure of interviewing Bella for my podcast and I encourage you to listen and encounter her positive spirit. You'll never look at difficulty in the same way again.

While I am humbled by Bella Picard and the inner-strength she has displayed, a big part of the journey back from my own injury was

---

21   Ibid.

22   Ibid.

refusing to give in to pain and impatience. Much of my recovery came by developing applications of the processes we have been exploring throughout the book. More and more, as I meditated and visualized, I was drawn back into those memories of when I had entered the zone during a performance. I've written elsewhere about the way I used to walk onto the field or when breaking the huddle, and I began to recapture that. I reentered that experience of feeling like I was the commander, like I'd returned to being the quarterback and I was the one in total control. I could feel the towel I kept in the front of my uniform pants while playing, that moment when I touched it and felt complete, ready, prepared to go into combat. I had learned to transform my mindset.

And while I was able to draw on past performances to get my mind right, one of the biggest things I had discovered was that I was not my performance. I had to see the difference between being an athlete and being more than an athlete—being Grant.

YOU ARE NOT YOUR PERFORMANCE. YOU ARE NOT YOUR INJURY. YOU ARE NOT YOUR MOST RECENT SETBACK.

You are not your performance. You are not your injury. You are not your most recent setback. We control the controllables. We show grit, refusing to give up. We come back. We learn and move on and try again. It's easy to become wrapped up in the image we think we hold for ourselves. If you are currently a bench player, you can't afford to let your time on the bench define you. If you've been a successful starter but suffered an injury or a reduction in your role, showing grit is about not letting the setback define you.

When we are injured, it's easy to think of ourselves as weak or lesser than we were before. Such thinking is a sure recipe for disaster. We end up giving into all the negatives. Instead, we should approach our mental comeback from injury with the same grit and intention as we do our physical rehab. One will help you get the other, and together they will get you back to the presence you need to succeed once again. In fact, there is even an opportunity when rehabilitating the body during injury to add to your game, to develop the mental performance we've been talking about and return stronger, more self-aware, more confident in the knowledge that you have faced adversity and gotten the better of it.

When your circumstance or your injury is a temporary setback, acknowledge it as such and stay steady in the work you do to improve your mental game. Prepare yourself so that when you get that second chance, or you return to physical health, you can excel. If your injury is season ending or career ending, then recognize that there will be many stages you will need to pass through as you prepare for what's next, even if that next is a new life path. It all starts by recognizing that the circumstances—the injury, aging, physical transformation—do not define you. Competitive athletes, even when they are hurt, are in the best shapes of their lives. Their bodies will be ready for them. And they have all the knowledge from having risen to the top to do so again when they return.

With events like serious injuries, we go through a multi-staged process that is largely parallel to what Elizabeth Kubler-Ross defined for grief: denial, anger, bargaining, depression, and acceptance. It's easy to get caught inside any one of these stages and become stuck there. The athlete often gets trapped in denial because of the way they have identified themselves by their performances. Every person's recovery from an injury or other forms of adversity will be unique and they will have different experiences throughout these stages, but we need to recognize that we must take the actions to make sure we continue to move forward through them and reach that place of acceptance or else we will not fully heal. What you will feel and experience along the way, while individualized, will be normal. Essentially, you must be willing to have a relationship with your injury, embrace the struggle, for it will be a struggle. But it's a struggle you can survive if you display grit. This may mean getting to the heart of the injury itself if it's chronic and understanding its cause, and it will certainly mean getting to the emotional root of how you react to it. The same is true of other kinds of setbacks, as well. What you see on the surface may not be the actual problem.

Along the way, as you recover or await your renewed opportunity, you've not only got to put in the mental reps, you've got to remain valuable to the culture you love. You can be the leader you were on the field while you are on the bench. You can give valuable advice to both those who are in the thick of competition and those who are training to meet their opportunity. You can be a cheerleader and a motivator, an example and a teammate. Staying "in the game" in all these ways will be essential to your return to performance. These are the traits that will keep you ready to be the next one up when you're given the green light, and they are the traits that will give others the confidence to continue to regard you as a leader.

COMEBACK STORIES

There are any number of famous comeback stories in sports, from Ben Hogan's recovery from a car accident, to Michael Jordan's spectacular return after he broke his foot and missed sixty-four games. Every fan could build a list of comeback favorites. One worth mentioning is Peyton Manning, arguably among the greatest quarterbacks in the history of the NFL. Manning missed the entire 2011 season following neck surgery on an injury that had troubled him for years. Over those years, he had put in performances most uninjured quarterbacks could never come close to realizing. His team, the Indianapolis Colts, despite his storied career to that point, responded to his yearlong absence by using their number one draft pick to choose quarterback Andrew Luck. Manning exercised his free agent option and signed with the Denver Broncos. And how did he respond to his return? In 2012 he put in a solid season, becoming the third quarterback in history to throw four hundred passes, the fastest to reach that mark, and named the AP NFL Comeback Player of the Year. A year later, he finished the season with fifty-five touchdown passes and a league-record 5,477 yards; he led the Broncos to being the first team to ever eclipse 600 points in a season and a Super Bowl appearance. And in 2015, he helped the Broncos win the Super Bowl L.

But perhaps no comeback story is as impressive as that of Lindsey Vonn, who, over the course of becoming the most decorated downhill skier in history with seventy-eight World Cup wins and an Olympic gold medal, has suffered a litany of injuries, several of which would have been career ending for most athletes. Between 2006 and 2016, she sustained nine major injuries and endured five surgeries, often forcing her to miss critical races and even a whole season. Here is but a partial list of the injuries she has suffered: two ACL tears, a fractured humerus that left her with a long plate and twenty screws, a concussion, a deep shin bruise, a severed tendon, etc. ... She competed in the PyeongChang Olympics wearing a back protector and a knee brace. One of her coaches, Chris Knight, said of her in advance of the PyeongChang games, "With everything she's come back from, it constantly amazes me that she has not backed off 1%." Anyone who knows Vonn will not be surprised at that, or surprised she won bronze in the downhill event. Writing about her in *Sports Illustrated*, Tim Layden said, "Vonn wants to show mastery of the compendium of injuries, heartbreaks, slights, embarrassments and missteps that have accompanied her 78 World Cup victories ... The lists of scars and of victories are intertwined: There might have been more of the latter had there been less of the former, but the meaning of the triumphs has been enriched by the struggles."[23]

Allowing your life and your mental strength to be enriched by struggle could be a definition of grit.

---

23   Tim Layden, "Lindsey Vonn's Scars Have Prepared Her for PyeongChang," *Sports Illustrated*, January 9, 2018, https://www.si.com/olympics/2018/01/09/lindsey-vonn-winter-olympics-2018-pyeongchang-injuries.

THE FEARFUL MIND

Fear of injury is probably one of an athlete's greatest worries and most damning distractions. That can be true whether you are trying to recover from injury and you fear its return or you are focused on the unknown potential for injury. The potential is always real. The problem is that you can't control it and you are limited in what you can do to prevent it. Being as prepared as you are capable of being, in mind and in body, in technique and in focus, allows you the few measures you have toward meaningful prevention. Applying such measures smartly is altogether different than focusing on what you can't know and can't control.

The other central fear nearly all athletes face (and all people for that matter), whether they will admit it or not, is the fear of failure. Like injury, the anticipation of failure is

FAILURE IS NOTHING MORE THAN A LEARNING DEVICE.

what causes the real harm. For actual failure is nothing more than a learning device. First, we must realize that the fear itself is not real. Craig Manning, PhD, in his book, *The Fearless Mind*, reminds us:

> What is fear? Can you show me fear? It's not possible, is it? We can only show the symptoms of fear; we cannot show fear itself. Fear doesn't exist in reality. It lives in our minds, in the abstract. Fear only exists in our thoughts of what may or may not happen in the future.[24]

If we apply the processes we've been turning to throughout this book, we can buttress ourselves against giving into this fixation on what we cannot control in much the same way we can help our bodies heal

---

24   Craig Manning, *The Fearless Mind* (Springville: Cedar Fort Press, 2010).

after injury. Because we're made up of energy, we can dictate the flow of our energy throughout our body alongside the flow of our blood. If you are really, truly tapping into the mind/body experience and you're breathing and you're meditating, you can direct energy for healing purposes to the parts of your body that are injured. It takes a great deal of practice to become proficient at this, but with diligence it is possible. What's much easier is to use the same techniques to direct positive energy to reduce and remove fear. If you truly want to be the next one up, then get meaningless fear out of your life. There's not a lion about to eat you, there are only opponents who might out-execute you on a given day, a busted play, a dropped ball, so get over it. Don't give into the fear. Talk to your fear. Direct your energy to rebound and recover and grow from adversity instead of living within the fearful mind. Remember what A.J. Andrews shared earlier in the book and realize that your fear is irrational.

When I went in for my original hip replacement, I didn't put myself in a good position to face the experience. I'd given into fear. I'd spent years locked in anger and depression. In preparation for the second surgery for the removal of the bone spur, I was meditating daily, I was visualizing being back inside a healthy body again, and I lifted myself up with positive affirmations. I had lost weight. I was mentally and physically the best I could be. All that preparation completely changed my rehabilitation because I was motivated and focused. I had firm intention. I knew the surgery was going to work, and I got myself ready to go and reunite with the person I had been before I viewed myself as an injured man.

CHAPTER 8

WHEN THE BUCK STOPS ...

Assuming a Leadership Role

Leaders aren't born, they are made. They are made
by hard effort, which is the price which all of us must
pay to achieve any goal which is worthwhile.

—Vince Lombardi

P eople want to be led. It's human nature. Teams need leaders. And leadership can come as easily from those who are "starters" as from those preparing for their time to shine in the spotlight. In fact, as the Vince Lombardi quotation that leads this chapters says, you'll never be a leader when you assume that primetime role unless you have developed the qualities of leadership as part of your preparation as the next one up. Often, leaders look like the second-string high school football safety I introduced you to in Chapter 2, a guy who was so consistent in his enthusiasm, his work ethic, and his care for his teammates that his peers elected him their captain.

Like that young man illustrates, leadership is a choice. It's not a title, position, or rank. You don't have to be named captain to be a leader. Leading is an attitude, one that exhibits the passion felt for the culture of the sport, the organization, and the team. The very act of making such a choice is one of intentionality. You must then back up intention with action.

Leadership can often be found among those who will be the next one up, because leading by example applies equally inside and outside of games. Its presence matters on the practice field and in the locker room. Leaders are the ones who stay after practice to work with others who want extra reps. Leaders start practice without waiting for the coach. They help the coach take notes after a practice or a game, they help them put away the equipment, they clean the practice facility or the locker room. They consistently demonstrate the grit of never giving up. When teammates lag during conditioning training, a leader runs alongside them, motivating them. A leader is your team's loudest cheerleader (or the quietest) and the first one to get in your face if you violate the principles of your team culture, or if you fail to give your best effort. Leaders embody the spirit of the team and through leading by example, they earn the trust of their team. People will buy into the culture you are helping to create by watching your actions.

> **LEADERSHIP IS A CHOICE. IT'S NOT A TITLE, POSITION, OR RANK.**

Sam Walker, the author *The Captain Class: A New Theory of Leadership*, talks about athletic leaders who sacrifice personal gain, recognition, and advantage for the good of other players and the good of the team. Among a few examples, Walker talks at length about Tim Duncan, the standout NBA player who spent his career with the San Antonio Spurs. Rather than trying to be a showman player or a stat leader (which he remained anyway because of his immense talent and work ethic), Duncan was famous for changing the roles he held on the team from year to year in order to accommodate the strengths brought to the team by new players. He was intent on making everyone around him better. He even once volunteered to take a pay cut to free up money to sign other players.

Writing about the style of leadership Duncan embodied, Walker said, "The great captains lowered themselves in relation to the group whenever possible in order to earn the moral authority to drive them forward in tough moments ... The easiest way to lead, it turns out, is to serve."[25]

As Walker tells us, and as Tim Duncan embodies, leadership is about others, not about the self. This chapter examines such a nature of leadership and will help you realize that leadership is always a choice, never selfish, and always 90 percent mental.

DAWN STALEY ON CREATING LEGACY LEADERSHIP

One of the few to break the stranglehold UConn has had on NCAA Women's basketball, Dawn Staley coached the University of South Carolina to the NCAA Championship in 2017, and later that year was named the head coach of US Women's Basketball. Staley, a

---

25   Sam Walker, *The Captain Class: A New Theory of Leadership* (New York: Random House, 2017).

former Virginia standout, Hall of Fame WNBA player, and three-time Olympic gold medalist. She also has an award named in her honor, the Dawn Staley Community Leadership Award, which is presented annually by the WNBA to the player who best exemplifies Staley's leadership, spirit, charitable efforts, and love for the game.

Staley has been deliberately creating what she labels "legacy leadership" actively developing the current generation of players to act on the principles of leadership established by the best leaders of the program's past. She not only coaches players on leadership, she creates opportunities for them to learn from alumni. Among the qualities Staley sees as critical for a leader are to demonstrate "respect for teammates," to become "great communicators," and to show they are never "afraid to make mistakes." She says when leaders "make a mistake, they own it."[26] Staley sees her college players as learning leadership lessons during their playing careers that they carry forward for the rest of their lives.

---

26 Molly Fletcher, "Episode 25—Dawn Stayley on Building a Championship Culture," November 16, 2017 in *Game Changers with Molly Fletcher*, podcast, MP3 audio, https://mollyfletcher.com/podcasts/dawn-staley-championship-culture/.

THE LANGUAGE OF LEADERSHIP

As important as leading by example, leaders must also have great communication skills. Whether that is communicating with coaches and bosses or players and colleagues, leaders must be adept at communicating clearly and honestly. There is a specific leadership language we can all learn, one that is built out of the self-talk we have already discussed. As a leader you have to speak in ways that replace words like "fear" and "hope" and "what if?" with "we can" and "we will" and "let's do it." It can take ten positive events to erase the effect of one negative verbal statement. Leaders must think equally about the message they want to convey and the language they will use to convey it.

Useful communication is down-to-earth and practical, not the stuff of raucous Hollywood halftime motivational speeches. There's no room for bull in the communication from leaders; they have to demand accountability, be intolerant of pessimism or blame, and expect toughness. Great leaders initiate team meetings to tackle issues of poor morale or needed motivation without the coaching staff being present.

I regularly called such meetings throughout my playing career. I think in my case, fulfilling such a role was instinctual, something in my nature or developed by watching people like my dad. But you can choose to have this sort of role. Moreover, not only do player-led meetings have a vital place in promoting the health of teams, there is an important equivalent in business environments. It's a recognition that meaningful leadership exists outside of an organizational chart or a nameplate. Part of why such outreach is successful is because it's all about leaders staying connected, really listening to others, and creating environments where people can have their say. When this happens, the group can check in, people can be heard, and a team can refocus on collective goals.

When I was completing an internship as a mental performance coach for my master's degree, I had the chance to watch the power of this in action. I was working with the football team at Junípero Serra High School. Serra is a school that is synonymous with producing elite athletes, graduating famous players like Tom Brady, Barry Bonds, Greg Jeffries, Lynn Swann, and John Robinson, among others. It is a place of high expectations. One day while I was working with the team, the coach stopped practice and spent forty-five minutes yelling at his players for their poor performance. None of the player-leaders knew what to do. This was the third day of my internship, but after I watched the player's confused reaction to the coach's tirade, I found one of the captains and said, "Why don't you take everybody into the locker room and have a player-led meeting?"

The guy looked at me with confusion and asked, "What do you want me to say?"

"What do you think you should say?"

"Tell them that this should never happen again," he said.

"Absolutely," I told him. "Get a dialogue going. Get them to buy into each other. Go in there, show them you are their leader. It might be uncomfortable, but get the team talking about how they will never put themselves in this position again."

The defensive coach saw me talking with this young man and asked me what I'd said. When I told him, he said, "Way to go, coach. That's exactly the kind of leadership we need from these kids."

People don't want to be managed, directed, or bossed around. They want to be led. Simon Sinek, a leadership expert and author of *Start with Why* and *Leaders Eat Last,* reminds us that "Bad leaders care about who is right, and good leaders care about what is right."[27] When your teammates see they can trust you, they know that you've got their backs, they see that you will never hold them accountable for something for which you would not hold yourself accountable, they are going to buy in. Great leaders not only reflect the organization's culture, they help define it and create it. If you want to operate in a culture where a third-string player holds another

PEOPLE DON'T WANT TO BE MANAGED, DIRECTED, OR BOSSED AROUND. THEY WANT TO BE LED.

player accountable for being late to weight training, then you must do your part to instill that belief in others. I've seen this example in action, and it's a powerful demonstration about the real nature of leadership. It is the sort of action that reveals the heart of a team's culture.

At halftime in the final game of my sophomore season at Chabot Junior College, we were losing 21–0 to a team that had been getting blown out all year, and our coach had told us, in pretty explicit terms involving some of our anatomical parts, what he'd thought of our performance. Then he and the rest of the coaching staff stormed out of the locker room. I and the rest of the captains spoke up and shouted, "We're not going to let our coach talk to us that way. And we're not going to let this team do this to us." The team got riled up and angry. We said, "Let's go do this. This is our last game." We reminded ourselves about what kind of culture we wanted to belong to. We took that anger and redirected its energy and went out and

---

27   Simon Sinek (@simonsinek), "Bad leaders care about who's right. Good leaders care about what's right," Twitter, March 29, 2013, https://twitter.com/ simonsinek/status/317615464622747648?lang=en.

beat that team 52–21.

Leaders set the standard of a culture, as the upperclassmen did in that game or as Douglas Conant did. Conant served as CEO of Campbell Soup Company. He turned a suffering company around, changing the culture by consciously putting the focus back on the people who worked there. He wrote 30,000 hand-written "thank-you" notes to his employees, an exercise that required that he pay attention to each and every person in the company. Conant's actions are similar to what PepsiCo CEO Indra Nooyi did for some of her employees. After visiting India to see her mother after she took the CEO position, she was humbled when a flood of people came to her mother's house to tell her what a good job she had done in raising such a successful daughter. Realizing her success really was due to her parents' belief in her, she wrote a letter to the parents of each of the members of her executive team, telling them what their child was doing at PepsiCo and thanking them for the gift of their child to her company.

These are powerful examples of positive, affirming expressions of leadership.

THE SCIENCE BEHIND LEADERSHIP: PAT SUMMITT

In a fascinating intertwining of science, business, and athletics, sports psychology researchers Andrea Becker and Craig Wrisberg, spent the 2004–2005 basketball season closely observing legendary coach Pat Summitt at work with her players. Summitt, who passed away in 2016, was the winningest coach in college basketball history. Long-regarded throughout the coaching community as a masterful leader and team-builder, Summitt was seen as an expert at maximizing the performances of her players.

Vanessa LoVerme Akhtar, a principal at a change management and strategy execution firm who also has a background in sports psychology, wrote about the findings of the Becker and Wrisberg study shortly after Summitt's death. Among those findings was this statistic: 48 percent of Summitt's behaviors during practice fell into the category of "instruction," most often instruction provided while the players were executing the skill she was teaching. When she did scold players, which was rare despite people's perception of Summitt as a taskmaster, she nearly always followed the correction with instruction. Akhtar, considering the importance of this finding for leaders in business, concluded, "… it's critical to provide on-the-job opportunities for learning, paired with real-time feedback—both positive and constructive. This enables employee growth which, in turn, will keep employees engaged and committed …."[28]

Drawing on the findings of the study, Akhtar also highlighted the importance of how often Summitt offered praise to her players. The researchers found that praise was the second most common practice Summitt used.

---

28 Vanessa LoVerme Akhtar, "What I Learned about Leadership from Pat Summitt," *Forbes*, June 8, 2016, https://www.forbes.com/sites/johnkotter/2016/07/08/what-i-learned-about-leadership-from-pat-summitt/#4cf941eb459a.

The study also included some fairly complex mechanisms for measuring if there were differences in how Summitt interacted with players who she had ranked as having high potential for development vs. those for whom she had lower expectations for growth. They found that Summitt provided the same quantity and quality of interactions with all her players. Drawing on this observation, Akhtar reminds leaders that they may be doing their employees a disservice if they treat those with high potential differently, writing, "In our work we continually see people across ranks and roles in organizations shine in unexpected ways when given the chance."[29]

We could all become better leaders by simply reading interviews with Pat Summitt or watching old game film of her coaching and observing how she interacted with her players, yet here's some science that bears out some of why her methods were so effective and how we might apply some of her approaches when asked to lead ourselves.

LEADERSHIP AS A CHOICE

In the instance of the game I described at Chabot, we chose to step up to our leadership roles. It is a daily choice to uphold that role. As you contemplate your leadership role, you need to ask yourself what kind of leader you want to be. What will be your leadership

---

29   Ibid.

style? Can you put a name to it? What will it look like? What does it feel like? I've heard the phrase "Leaders take the stairs," which to me suggests a number of things at once: just like going to work each day and choosing to get on the elevator or to take the stairs, leaders make a conscious choice; there's real work involved because leadership never offers the easy path; you earn the climb rather than having something handed to you; and you're always setting an example by even the simplest actions. You earn the opportunity to lead, but then you have to make a choice on a daily basis to uphold the position of leadership.

Once you have assumed the choice of rising to leadership, then people will look to you. There's a responsibility you must live up to. That's why great leaders never lose their breath. They have mastered all the processes we have talked about in this book so that they can maintain a posture of poise, confidence, and control. When you exhibit a strong sense of control, your team is better able to follow suit. When they look in their leader's eyes and see belief and readiness, they will find the will to believe in themselves and in the power of the team to overcome whatever adversity they may face.

Leadership is within you. You must make the choice to embrace it and go about the preparation that will allow you to succeed. Coaches and bosses go looking for those who possess the traits of leadership; they scour teams in search of leaders, and as a result, the move as the next one up is often a move based on acknowledgement of the leadership you have demonstrated and awareness of your ability to sustain the actions demanded of leadership.

CHAPTER 9

HOW THE PROS PROCESS THE UNKNOWN

Owning The "It" Factor

If you want to be the best, you have to be willing to do the things other people aren't willing to do.

—*Michael Phelps, winner of twenty-eight Olympic medals (the most of all time), swimming*

In sports, we often refer to very best as having the "it" factor. Or sometimes we refer to these nearly otherworldly athletes as having "the total package." I once had a coach who talked about certain players as being "gold nugget studs." Those with the "it" factor possess the intangibles we so often associate with athletes of the highest caliber. All of these expressions recognize that there are some individuals who seem to excel at levels that even other gifted athletes can't quite reach. There's no doubt that every sport sees the occasional superstar participant who transforms their sport in ways that shatter expectations and leave a permanent mark, athletes like Serena Williams, Mia Hamm, Michael Jordon, Tiger Woods, and Joe Montana. And while I absolutely do see the transformative power of such complete, elite competitors, my own take on the "it" factor is different: I prefer to see "it" as an acronym for "intelligently tenacious," or "intelligent tenacity."

In developing "intelligent tenacity," we will learn the best means to attaining supreme confidence and see the value of cultivating mentors, near and far, to help us achieve our goals.

IT = INTELLIGENT TENACITY

My view of intelligent tenacity allows room for the mindfulness and commitment expressed by such gifted athletes. It does not disregard their talent, but it gives recognition to the intentionality of their choice to excel and the work they have put in to achieve success. When I think about an intelligently tenacious person, I can't help but remember how Phil Jackson, the legendary coach of the Chicago Bulls, once brought George Mumford in to teach his team mindfulness. Michael Jordan, upon seeing the effects of mental training on his performance, said he didn't want George to work with anyone else for fear he might lose the edge it provided him. Eventually, Jordan reached levels of physical performance where he saw all the challenges and growth available to him in the mental aspects of the game.

Jordan recognized the advantage he gained from developing a daily meditation practice and employing many of the mindfulness techniques we have explored throughout the book. Mumford, in turn, went with Jackson when he took over coaching duties with the LA Lakers, and the results of Mumford's work with Kobe Bryant paralleled what Jordan had accomplished. Bryant, another one of the handful of players in basketball history who forever transformed the game, has said of working with Mumford that, he "helped me understand the art of mindfulness. To be neither distracted or focused, rigid or flexible, passive or aggressive. I learned just to be."[30] That "just be" philosophy helped Bryant lead the Lakers to five NBA titles.

ACCESSING YOUR CONFIDENT SELF

Like Jordan and Bryant, intelligently tenacious athletes have a presence they carry within them, one that my mentor, Graham Betchart, discusses when he talks about athletes who reach a level he labels "supreme confidence." Graham teaches us that confidence is an action, not a feeling, Supremely confident athletes have worked so diligently on mental reps that instead of acting out of fear or anxiety, they choose to live out the right action by talking themselves into

---

30   Kobe Bryant, "George Mumford: Mindfulness and Performance Expert," George Mumford, accessed March 5, 2019, https://georgemumford.com/home_draft/.

"factual space."[31] As we have discussed, Graham suggests that rather than responding to emotion, we gain confidence in our preparation and in the knowledge that we have performed well in the past, then once we repeat positive actions and positive self-talk over and over in our daily regimens, we gain confidence we don't have to think about and can draw on in any situation. Doug Collins, who coached Michael Jordan when they were with the Washington Wizards late in Jordan's career (Jordan was forty-one and part owner and general manager as well) tells a story of a night when Jordan missed eleven shots in a row. He then made a shot just before Collins brought him to the bench late in a game. When Jordan asked Collins why he was pulling him out. Collins said, "Michael, you just missed eleven shots in a row."

Jordan's reply was, "But I made the last one."[32] That's supreme confidence. Jordan knew, without a doubt, that even at forty-one, he could hit the next shot when called upon, just as he had done throughout his career.

MICHAEL JORDAN AND MENTAL TOUGHNESS

Doug Collins, who coached Michael Jordan in the last two years of his professional career with the Washington Wizards, told a story on the ESPN *Mike and Mike Show* that captures Jordan's intelligent tenacity. When

---

31   Graham Betchart, "Learn It: Pillar 3: Supreme Confidence," June 19, 2017, video, https://www.youtube.com/watch?v=txHQKsnk2_o.

32   "The Psychopathic Mindset of Michael Jordan," May 17, 2017, https://www.youtube.com/watch?v=DjRbobUjAt8.

Jordan was forty-one, still playing at a level that could match anyone in the NBA, Collins pulled him from a game against the Indiana Pacers when they were trailing by twenty-five points at the end of the third quarter. Collins told Jordan, "Look, I know you think we can still win this game, and if we make a run and get back in it, I'll put you in, but we've got big games coming up." The Wizards went on to lose. Only after the game was Collins informed that Jordan only had eight points in the game, which broke a streak of well more than eight hundred games in which he had scored in double figures. The media went crazy, wondering how Collins could show such disrespect for a legendary player by allowing the streak to come to an end.

Collins went on to tell how, on the bus trip to the airport that night, Jordan asked Collins to scoot over and sat next to him. He looked at his coach and asked, "Do you think I can still play?"

Collins told him, "Absolutely."

Jordan said, "You know, to be my coach you have to believe in me and believe that I can still play."

Collins told him, "Michael, I believe in you."

Jordan replied, "You did the right thing tonight. I don't care about the points, but I needed to know that you believed in me."

The team flew home, arriving at 3:30 in the morning.

At 7:30 a.m., Jordan was in the fitness room working out. The next night, they played the New Jersey Nets. By this point in his career, Jordan had a bad knee, and that night he was playing with a deep cut on his finger that didn't allow him to straighten it. Jordan scored on his first three shots of the game. At a time-out, he told his coach, "I want the ball right there the rest of the game," he said, while pointing to a spot on the floor. "Don't take me out until I tell you." With two minutes left in the game, he gave Collins the signal to remove him. Jordan seemed to score at will throughout the game. When he approached the bench, Collins asked him what had happened that night. Jordan, in the spirit of the competitive warrior, told him that player who was guarding him had confided that his back was hurting and he was struggling. Jordan said, "Don't ever tell me that you've got a problem. I'll make you pay for that."

Jordan, at age forty-one, scored fifty-one points that night. He scored forty-six points in the next game. After scoring ninety-seven points in two nights, Jordan looked at Doug Collins and said, "I told you I could still play." Collins said he had never seen an example of mental toughness and competitive will that surpassed that experience of coaching Michael Jordan.[33]

---

33   Ibid.

As you are aware from the stories of this book, like most athletes, I'm a huge sports fan, whether a fan of Michael Jordan or hundreds of other inspiring athletes. As much as I like watching the performances of great athletes, I also love hearing them talk about their lives and experiences, and about their habits. I'm fortunate. Because of my work, I not only get to help athletes grow in confidence and mindfulness, I get to interview athletes from nearly every sport on my podcast, *90% Mental*. Among hundreds of topics, we often discuss the linkage between tenacity and confidence.

Intelligent tenacity is a mindset that can lead us to supreme confidence. It requires combining factual intelligence and emotional intelligence. Think of it as a balanced scale of IQ and EQ. We not only have developed the tools to push aside negative emotions and use that energy to produce positive actions, we've set about training in a purposeful manner, whether that is the approach we take to our MVPs and BVTs or it's the work of studying our opponents, knowing the game plan, helping our teammates, or adding value to the culture of our organization. It's about paying homage to your upbringing inside and outside of the culture, which means both paying tribute to parents, mentors, coaches, and teammates, and about honoring the discipline and commitment you've learned along the way. Intelligent tenacity is about doing the right thing all the time.

MENTORS NEAR AND FAR

In this spirit of seeking mentorship, an intelligently tenacious person knows they not only need to honor the people and processes that have got them to where they are, they need to find and cultivate mentors to grow. This applies to those immediately around you bringing positive influences into your life, but also finding and studying those who can provide outstanding models at a distance and from the past. How have the elite performers arrived where they have? What mental preparation techniques do they use? How do they develop an intelligently tenacious mind?

One big mistake we make is to believe that those we typically associate with the ordinary usage of the "it factor"—those superstars we all know by name—don't face adversity. The opposite is true. The highest achievers regularly face adversity. It kind of goes hand in hand with the demands of performing at high levels, when your body and your mind are taxed to the maximum, competitions are numerous, frequent, elite, and expectations are high. As a result, such elite performers are regularly the targets of competitors, the media, and critics alike. At the same time, they are often battling injury, fatigue, boredom, and expectations of perfection. Don't forget, starters are expected to (and expect to) start. Yet simply playing at high levels with frequency is demanding. There are 162 games in a Major League Baseball regular season; eighty-two games in an NBA season plus the addition of playoff games; a championship caliber tennis player will play at least five matches to reach the finals of a Grand Slam and will play, on average, fifteen tournaments a year. None of this counts practice time. Or media demands. Or travel. You get the picture. Elite performers need good mental performance strategies to cope with all the stress they face. Some of the best make excellent models to study when you are developing your own mental performance strategies no matter where you are in your career.

One excellent model is the woman many regard as the best tennis player of all time, Serena Williams. She has said, "My game is my mental toughness. Just not only to be able to play, to win, but to be able to come back when I'm down. Both on the court and after tough losses, just to continue to come back and continue to fight, it's something that takes a lot of tenacity."[34] Williams uses her tenacious approach to the game to develop a mental calm that allows her to focus and find internal strength. The advice she gives herself can apply to any of us. In a 2015 video she completed for *Sports Illustrated*, she explained, "When I am behind in a game, that's when I become the most relaxed because I realize, usually, it's not going to get any worse than this. You have nothing to lose at that point, and someone with nothing to lose can be a very dangerous opponent." Her strategy when playing from behind is to apply a WIN mindset and focus on one point at a time. "Focus on one point and then the next one, only as they come."[35]

> **"WHEN I AM BEHIND IN A GAME, THAT'S WHEN I BECOME THE MOST RELAXED BECAUSE I REALIZE, USUALLY, IT'S NOT GOING TO GET ANY WORSE THAN THIS."**

Williams has applied this same WIN approach when battling larger adversity. Sadly, she's been attacked by the media for speaking her mind, she's been the victim of racial slurs, her physique has been questioned, even her choice of outfits comes under scrutiny. She's had to overcome tremendous challenges, both physically and as a victim of the media sensation that has attached itself to her, including the difficulty of her return to tennis a year after giving birth. After winning 2017's Australian Open in the early stages of her pregnancy, she later

---

34 Patrick Cohn, "'My Game is My Mental Toughness' Says Serena Williams," Sports Psychology for Tennis, October 5, 2017, https://www.sportspsychologytennis.com/my-game-is-my-mental-toughness-says-serena-williams/.

35 "Serena Williams explains the art of a comeback," *Sports Illustrated*, May 12, 2015, https://www.si.com/tennis/video/2015/05/12/serena-williams-art-of-comeback.

nearly died while delivering her daughter, suffering a pulmonary embolism. As if the recovery from near death and pregnancy wasn't enough, because of the rules governing international women's tennis (despite being ranked number one in the world when she departed the game for maternity leave), she was ranked number 453 when she competed in her first Grand Slam event upon her return at the French Open, meaning she would have to play all the world's top-ranked players in her first matches. The outrage of the policy that ranked her as an unseeded player sparked a rule change, allowing her to enter Wimbledon as the twenty-fifth ranked player and the US Open as a seventeen seed. She advanced to the finals in both.

We would be hard-pressed to find a better mentor than someone like Serena Williams. She's not just an athlete who possesses the "it factor" on the tennis court, she lives by the credo of intelligent tenacity.

THE DECEPTION OF "LUCK"

Studying the preparation techniques and processes of athletes like Serena Williams and Michael Jordan can prove instructive to all of us. What you quickly realize is that when you reach their level of competitiveness, it is almost entirely the mental game that separates the greats from the rest. However, it's easy to look at the very best athletes in the world and think they were merely lucky along their path to success or that their life lessons don't apply to us. We can look at them, see them as having the "total package," and view them only as something to aspire to. But the applications we can take from them go far beyond creating aspirations. It is easy to think that a second stringer or bench player can't possess the total package. Can you, working hard but finding yourself a third string selection, have the "it factor"? Like a lot of things, it's entirely your own decision whether you think all those with "it" are already starting or you believe "it" is a combination of the right attitude, proper dedication, possession of physical and mental talents, application of communication skills, and demonstration of an ability to be

IT IS ALMOST ENTIRELY THE MENTAL GAME THAT SEPARATES THE GREATS FROM THE REST.

resilient in difficult circumstances. Don't ever let someone's rank or position push you down a level and not allow you to see that you have intentionally developed the elements of the "it factor."

Because I have a belief system that views "it" in the terms by which I have defined intelligent tenacity, I refuse to believe in luck—good luck or bad. I believe there is actually a danger to giving into superstition, whether that is a belief in a single good or bad game, or it is a mindset that believes those who have "it" simply were lucky, born with the right genetic attributes, provided the right lucky breaks. Such belief systems discredit the work the individual has put in. They diminish the value of their reps—physical and mental—and remove the athlete's accountability. What happens to your confidence if you've been playing a sport for eleven, thirteen, or fifteen years and you have a bad game? Does that mean it was just a bad game and, as a Buddhist might say, "what is so is so," or do you just think you were unlucky? If you take the latter view, what does that do to your confidence? And think about the opposite. You've been working hard, earning opportunity and respect, gaining playing time—do you want that dismissed as "lucky?" You've worked so hard for so long, doesn't a vision of luck cheapen your accomplishment? Instead of thinking about luck, we are far better off to put stock in the work to become our own best "total package." If you have a bad play or a bad game, put confidence in the work you've done and apply the processes we have explored—honor and embrace your process and get your mental strategies in place.

When you abandon dependency on things like luck, you instead develop the real material of preparation. A confident mind is a prepared mind. There's a huge difference between being scared of a situation because you know you've not done the work and simply being afraid because you have entered the unknown. "It" athletes like Serena Williams are never unprepared. She can face the unknown precisely because she's learned how to be ready for it. We are all human, so we will all face emotion—fear, frustration, uncertainty. But when we know with total confidence that we've done all we can to be ready, then we have the tools in place to let go of the emotion or even channel its energy and take care of the task at hand.

A DOG STORY

Sometimes the needs of stepping into the unknown, staring down the fear, and choosing to control what we can control can come in the most ordinary of times, including those outside of competition and challenging work environments. Those needs can arrive even when you're doing something as simple as walking your dog. Realizing the power of our ability to shape the moment and control our actions came to me in just such an ordinary way.

I was, quite literally, walking my dogs. I have two small dogs, eleven pounds and sixteen pounds, and one blissful Saturday morning under clear, beautiful skies, I was walking them in an open space behind my house, casually drinking my coffee and enjoying the rarefied beauty of looking all the way across the length of the Bay

Bridge below me and into the East Bay.

I looked fifty yards up the path and saw an unleashed large, muscular Pit Bull Terrier. I love all dogs and believe Pit Bulls have gotten a bad rap by those who have stereotyped the whole breed due to the negligence of a few unethical owners, but this dog was unleashed and in a low stance staring straight at us, its athletic body looking like a runner about to explode out of the blocks. Seeing him, despite his beauty, I felt an energy present and I could not help but think of coaches I'd had who, applying the stereotype of an aggressive reputation, used to refer to their toughest athletes as Pit Bulls, encouraging them toward ruthlessness in their play. It was an ordinary moment of facing the unknown, and the dog could be just another pet out for a happy walk with its owner or it could be thinking my little dogs looked like a nice breakfast.

My dogs were oblivious to its presence, busy sniffing along the trail. I was watching the dog, wondering what it might do, and I went right into my breath and told myself everything's cool. I exhaled and then I breathed again and suddenly the dog took off down the hill and straight for us.

Now this is the moment of chaos I've been talking about throughout the book, the kind of moment begging our minds to react with an emotional response. And, as is always the case in such moments, I was faced with a choice. I could give in to the emotion and panic. I could react instinctively and pick up my dogs and hold them to me, potentially opening myself to injury should the Pit Bull attack. Or I could choose to remain calm in the face of the unknown.

I took a breath, allowed calm to flood through my body, and I let the dog come to us. I leaned into the moment. My dogs, slow to recognize the dog coming at them, finally heard him and growled. The Pit Bull arrived and growled in response. I felt utterly calm. I talked in a calming puppy-verbalizing kind of way, saying, "It's all right, guys. It's okay." I allowed the positive energy I was feeling to travel down the leashes. I maintained my breath, sat in the calm I felt. Then I tugged gently on the leashes, leading my dogs away. The Pit Bull lost interest.

The moment was over. The unknown had revealed itself. Turning and walking away, it felt for a moment like my knees wanted to buckle, that typical adrenaline spike when you face a moment of fear. But my breath had saved me. I can never actually know if I was in danger or if taking control of my emotions altered what might have happened. That's the very nature of the unknown. I can only know that I made a choice, that I chose not to give into emotion and instead to fall back on the mental performance practice I've been doing for years. I controlled what I could control.

We're all going to have moments like this. Will we take control over how we react to them? Will we draw on our preparation when we face being asked to step up our role at work or when we are provided the chance to step into the heat of competition? The choice is ours to make. If we want to reap the rewards of developing our own "it factor," we must put in the work, develop clear intention, and act.

If you adopt and implement the best practices *The Next One Up Mindset* has outlined, I am confident you will make yourself whole and ready for the moment when you are called upon, and that you will find and develop the processes that allow you to approach your goals with intelligent tenacity.

THE NINE BEST PRACTICES OF THE NEXT ONE UP MINDSET:

1. Turn Crisis into Opportunity

2. Embrace Your Role

3. Discover Confidence in Preparation

4. Quiet the Inner Critic

5. Train the Subconscious Mind

6. Release Your Inner Warrior

7. Apply Grit for Overcoming Adversity

8. Assume a Leadership Role

9. Own the "It" Factor

CHAPTER 10

THE CORPORATE ATHLETE

Next One Up Applications in the Workplace

I spent seventeen years developing a lucrative corporate career with ever-increasing responsibilities. Within that career, I moved companies, changed positions, grew sales territories, implemented new processes, and brought new products to market. Over those years I did everything from working as a recruiter to selling state-of-the-art equipment to some of the largest data center companies in the world. I was very good at what I did and I became quite successful. In my own instance, neither the work or the rewards consistently brought me happiness, which is why I left traditional corporate life, formed Gameface Performance, and embarked on the work that has been the focus of *The Next One Up Mindset*. I'm not suggesting that you follow suit and quit your job, but I absolutely do believe that, in a world of demanding responsibilities and high expectations, corporate life is best captured by the term "corporate athlete."

Many of the demands we face at work are not so different than those faced by high-caliber athletes. Certainly, the need for mental toughness in the face of chaos is similar. There are a thousand competitive elements in the ordinary lives in business. Think about it; the very act of applying and interviewing for your first job required entering a competitive mindset because someone else (probably many others) wanted that job, too. My belief that businesspeople, particularly those in, or ascending toward, senior positions are corporate athletes is

MANY OF THE DEMANDS WE FACE AT WORK ARE NOT SO DIFFERENT THAN THOSE FACED BY HIGH-CALIBER ATHLETES.

a recognition that participating in sports is about far more than any physical aspects. Participating in athletics teaches tenacity, teamwork, leadership, communication, and confidence. It also demands development of emotional intelligence (EQ), which is equally vital in the corporate world where you must constantly monitor the energy you feel from others you work with, read their body language, and hear their vision and ideas. In short, EQ helps create real teamwork. These are among the reasons I view my participation in sports as having been the greatest influence in my success in the corporate world. Taken together, these experiences have led me to the pleasure of working with several businesspeople in times of transition through an executive boot camp that I co-facilitate alongside some brilliant business coaches in San Francisco. These leaders are in the midst of facing a whole new unknown.

The boot camp applies the principles you've found throughout this book in a corporate setting at the most daunting times of the participants' lives—when they have experienced job changes, layoffs, retirement, advancement, and other such circumstances. I do hope you've found value, inspiration, and application for your work environment within the ideas and processes throughout the book. This chapter builds on some of those ideas in ways that can specifically be applied as a corporate athlete. But at the center of any workplace applications are the core processes we've talked about because the natural state of all high-level work environments requires you to venture into the unknown constantly. Whether you are dealing with moody or unpredictable people, changing processes, impromptu requests, changing leadership, or shifts in company direction, the unknown is everywhere. You'll never learn to face it effectively until you apply the processes and ideas we have discussed in the preceding chapters. But this chapter can act as a handy return point when you're facing something at work that requires you to be at your mental best.

A CORPORATE WARRIOR IN BATTLE

Sometimes the stakes of change and venturing into the unknown are huge. But the decisions remain the same. No one exemplifies the courage and the difficulty of such decisions better than my friend and former colleague, Tony Peil. Tony had been with my company, Wesco Distribution, for about six months when I transitioned out of the corporate world to start Gameface Performance. He was extremely experienced and quite successful, having spent seventeen years in the larger industry, but with only six months on the job at Wesco Distribution, Tony was still learning the culture, personalities, and back office procedures of the company. I'd been with them for seven and a half years, starting in a sales role where I'd been given a newly formed sales territory in the Bay area and had grown that territory from zero dollars in sales to over $20 million in annual sales. We sold essentially everything except for the servers to global data centers. With my success, I'd moved into something closer to a global account management role servicing those end users I'd acquired. Despite it being a very lucrative position, I had decided to pursue my passions rather than continue in this position.

It was actually Tony's sister-in-law, who I was training to replace me. She had been with Wesco Distribution for a couple of years after a career in the telecom industry, so she was still learning the ins and outs of distribution and was shocked at the size of the sales she would be guiding. She and I had a smooth, lengthy, and robust transition period working together, and right after Christmas I held my last transition meeting with her and a client, then departed for Lake Tahoe for ten days of vacation. I hadn't been back in town for too many days when I received a phone call from Tony, saying he wanted to tell me about his sister-in law. I assumed something was up at work, but Tony told me that, about ten days after I left, she had sought medical attention and was diagnosed with an extremely rare and deadly flu virus. She had slipped into a coma.

The doctors gave Tony's sister-in-law a 5 percent chance of survival, and if she did survive, she might not have much quality of life. I asked Tony what I could do to help, and he told me "Just be there for me, man. I need someone to talk to." She passed away a few days later. Tony was overwhelmed with the loss of his sister-in-law and trying to comfort his wife. And then, in the midst of his mourning, the company told him that they hoped he would consider taking over my old territory in addition to keeping his own and take advantage of his long experience in the industry. Tony didn't know what to do.

We spoke a few times on the phone and then got together for beers to talk it through. He told me, "I don't know what to do. They're all asking me to step up as a leader because of my experience, but I'm still trying to learn all this crap. People are quitting. What am I supposed to do? I don't know if I'm ready for this." We talked for a while. I heard the pain and uncertainty in his voice. I listened to him closely.

In the end, I said, "You can do two things. If you know that mentally you can't do this right now because you need to go mourn, that's totally fair and it's right for you to tell them you're not prepared in the state of mind you're naturally in right now. That's okay. It's your decision to make. Your other option, if you can see the opportunity, is to fight through the pain, honor your sister-in-law heroically and chose to step up. You show your mental toughness, grit, resiliency, presence, leadership, competence, all of that, to the team. You can, if you want, rise above this and show yourself and everybody else that you're bulletproof. You have to make that choice. It's up to you."

Tony chose to accept the challenge and face the unknown. He's succeeded and even thrived. We've talked several times and it hasn't, of course, been at all easy, but Tony offers a stunning example of choosing to turn crisis into opportunity.

TURNING CRISIS INTO OPPORTUNITY

The only constant in business is change. In the high-tech sector of the Bay area, whole product lines change overnight. I can't tell you how many times I received a call at 3:00 p.m. to place an order the customer wanted filled that day, and how many calls that resulted in when I had to draw on cultivated relationships to make sure their wishes—often multimillion-dollar orders—were fulfilled. Or how many times, when I worked as a recruiter, I worked impossible hours and called in every contact I'd ever made to find the candidate who checked all the most impossible boxes only to discover they were quietly fielding another offer. Such scenarios are the ordinary purview of business. You constantly face the unknown and you frequently encounter crisis: your boss quits, your best contact at your biggest contract goes on maternity leave, your company reorganizes and consolidates divisions. How do you react? Do you panic?

Or maybe the stakes appear much smaller: you've just finished research on a new project, shared it with your boss, who is so impressed with your findings that he asks you to present them to the leadership team. With twenty minutes notice! In that moment, the stakes don't seem small at all. Do you let the intimidation of the circumstance knock you off your game? Or do you breathe, draw on your preparation, trust in your abilities, allow a moment to envision how you want the presentation to go, remind yourself you are ready to go knock it out of the park? Ultimately, the choice is yours.

Just as athletes prepare physically and mentally to become starters, if you are looking to advance your career and take on more responsibility, your opportunities will likely come at a time of crisis. Will you rise to the occasion? Can you see opportunity when everyone else sees uncertainty? To do so requires both a conscious choice and an ability to think in patterns opposite those of most. When others react with fright—and respond with fight or flight—you can choose mental might.

EMBRACING YOUR ROLE

Just as every crisis has an opportunity, every team requires people who fulfill their roles and every role has room for a star. No one in business isn't part of a team. Part of embracing your role is recognizing that the team needs are bigger than your own. That doesn't mean you can't embrace your part, quite the opposite. If you are the understudy, then study; be the best understudy there ever was. If you are an assistant manager aspiring to be a manager, or a vice president aspiring to be president, the superior course to achieving your aspiration is to be the best assistant manager or vice president you are capable of being. Rock your role. Study the strengths, weaknesses, and practices of those in higher roles you admire and learn from them. Seize every small opportunity along the way, and you'll be fully prepared for advancement when it comes. Serve your team well and they'll serve you well.

Those who only focus on the unknown, even if that unknown is leveled on their dreams about holding a higher position, are doing themselves no favors. The real work is in preparation. It's no different than worrying about the next play or the next possession. Rather than worry, do the work to be ready, then take your breath, visualize, and tell yourself you are ready. If you've given everything you have to your present role, then you really are ready.

TRAINING THE SUBCONSCIOUS MIND

WIN IN THE WORKPLACE

Such processes nearly always start with adopting a WIN mindset. The corporate athlete can easily become overwhelmed with commitments and projects and must actively live within a "What's important now?" approach. Just like in any kind of performing environment, there are so many distractions, so even when you are on-task and productive, a thousand interruptions challenge for your attention—internal meetings, conference calls, water cooler drama—it all flashes at you like deer on the side of the highway demanding your notice. Whenever there appears too much to accomplish, you must go back to a WIN attitude and determine what actually needs your attention. Sometimes you literally have to get your breath, and you always have to get your breath metaphorically, establish a hierarchy of tasks and determine what matters most to accomplishing long-term goals. The WIN mindset in this application corresponds quite directly to remembering "what is your why?" Why are you doing this in the first place? What's the goal? What's your role? Is everyone in agreement on why they are taking the actions that they are? How does the one thing fit into the bigger picture of the real thing—the mission or the project goal?

VISUALIZATION AND SELF-TALK FOR WORK

Just as leaders need to know their intentions if they are to act on them, there are lots of opportunities to apply the processes of this book at work. Chief among these is visualization. My work now frequently requires me to do public speaking. I never speak without first visualizing myself performing and the audience's reaction. It might be a lengthy, developed, and detailed visualization or just a quick second before responding to someone's request, but I always see the performance as I wish it to go. And after the visualization I will say something to myself to secure my intention. In my case, I try never to speak without acknowledging the joy I feel at getting to do what I do for a living. That's a part of a mindset we can all act on, recognizing that we *get* to do things rather than have to do them. In my case, I really do find joy in my work with others, so acknowledging that joy is a way of giving thanks, at the same time it is a means to take the stage with energy and a smile on my face. How different might your work be if you were to see opportunity in everything required of you rather than duty? Take the processes of *The Next One Up* and bring them to work with you. See yourself performing with energy and confidence; pump yourself up with positive talk. Then walk into your office or that meeting with your head high, your shoulders back, and a smile beaming. How might the energy of the room be changed? What if we all approached our work with the spirit and energy we bring to the joy we find in athletics and recreation? How different would our lives be if we did?

These are just a few applications to focus on at work that apply mental preparedness principles. From them and from other parts of this book, find your own way and your own applications.

APPLYING GRIT IN THE FACE OF ADVERSITY

Because people are people—with all their moods and contradictions—and because you can't conduct business without people, you are going to face adversity. And because business demands are constantly changing, you have to be flexible. If you remain rigid every day on the job, at some point you're going to break.

I can't help but think of all the people at Apple who reported directly to Steve Jobs. Imagine working for someone who could change course on design after months of work, who demanded everyone be at their best always, and who could fly off the handle into fits of rage. Reading about Jobs reminds me of a few coaches I've known. Think of the grit it takes to stay on in such a circumstance. How many times must his employees have wanted to tell him off? Sometimes simply dealing with such people takes a warrior mentality and a bamboo approach. You must be able to adapt and adjust. You have to know when it is the right moment to stand your ground and when to let things roll off your back. Knowing your why is key to making such a decision, because knowing your why really means an ability to look past the moment and recall how and where the immediate need—whether that's confronting a peer, standing up to a boss, or helping the customer—fits into the larger objective.

A big part of assuming a warrior mentality in the workplace is realizing you have choices to make when it comes to empowering yourself. When you are working the corporate grind, it's easy to get stuck—in a position, or in an attitude, or both. You might think the role you currently have is all you can achieve. Some people get on the treadmill of working really hard but not working smart. When you're stuck it's hard to see opportunities or find the energy to put yourself in positions where you will get noticed. Feeling stuck in these ways only adds to your stress. But remember, feeling stuck is exactly that, a feeling. What can you control? You can control your attitude. You can control your preparation. You can decide whether you can seek a new role within your organization or look outside of it. You can choose to further your education or take on additional responsibilities that can expose you to other strengths, talents, and opportunities.

A BIG PART OF ASSUMING A WARRIOR MENTALITY IN THE WORKPLACE IS REALIZING YOU HAVE CHOICES TO MAKE WHEN IT COMES TO EMPOWERING YOURSELF.

There are external sources of stress as well that create an adverse atmosphere, the stress you feel when your department has missed its number, or you've missed your sales quota, or you've suffered a mass exodus of talent and the team has lost much of its institutional knowledge as a result. Think back over the past year of your work life; how many things happened during that year that were never predicted in sales projections, strategic plans, or budgets? Crisis, or what seems like crisis, happens with surprising regularity. These are the times when you must call on your inner warrior. You've not only got to step up to battle during difficult circumstances, you've got to find innovation to take on problems. You can't do either if you give yourself over to the stress and succumb to emotion. In such times you must draw on your mental performance reserves, talk yourself through it, trust that you've been in tight spots before and you have the tools to fight your way through difficulty. Bend with the situation when required and find a new tactic.

Calling on your inner warrior for many feels like calling on the aggressive parts of yourself. That's not what I'm talking about. As Chapter 6 made clear, drawing on your warrior spirit isn't about aggression, it's about mindfulness. In the workplace, to an even greater extent than on the playing field, performance is about the mental game. The pressures are less overt, the chaos less obvious. But pressure and chaos are always lurking, and the mindful corporate athlete possesses the tools required to handle both.

ASSUMING THE LEAD

Whether you are leading from a position of authority or demonstrating leadership skills "from the rear" as it were, doing your best at all times—leading by example for how work should be done, showing enthusiasm and trustworthiness—will help establish a culture that lifts everyone up. Showing leadership when you don't have a formal title allows you to develop and practice the skills you'll need when an opportunity arises and offers evidence that you're the one to fulfill that opportunity. I'm not suggesting that you undercut your boss or overstep your role, only that you examine the qualities of leadership you place value on and exemplify them in your work. This also means seizing opportunity whenever it's presented, whether that is taking a formal role when offered, being the one others come to with questions, or simply saying yes when someone in authority asks to take the reins on a special project. More than likely, your work will get noticed and it will pay off. Even if it doesn't in an overt way and your boss takes credit for your work, you'll still benefit from the implementation of your idea and will have gained the experience of doing new work to add to your toolbox.

To truly be a leader means waking up with intention, knowing no matter what your role is, you need to be purposeful, and you must want to be the best version of you within that environment. Just as I encouraged athletes do earlier in the book, this means writing your intentions down, talking them out in your self-talk, and identifying what your intention looks like and feels like. And then if you have time on your commute or in some other moment outside work, start to exercise your mantras and your positive self-talk, so the moment you shut your car door or step off the train you're ready to execute. Give yourself direction for your day and, like the athlete ready to execute a play, you can carry your intentionality into your work.

BREATHING FOR BALANCE

Preparing for the Next Opportunity and Finding Harmony

This book has been all about preparing for the unknown. One central premise is that the unknown always contains opportunity. Whether you are practicing to prepare for a starting role as an athlete or you are working your way up to a leadership position in a corporate setting, you have committed to putting in the work to achieve clear goals. Not hopes. Goals. Defined, achievable goals that require effort and readiness.

If you put the processes of *The Next One Up Mindset* to work for you, you'll have a playbook for achieving those goals and for seizing opportunity whenever it presents itself. Part of the beauty of practicing mindfulness and participating in mental skills training is that it not only results in success in the venture that has been your focus, you also emerge a happier, healthier individual in mind and body. More important still, the work you do bleeds over into the rest of your life. You will feel more balanced and able to find the harmony between your professional endeavors and your private life.

With those deep calming breathes, you learn to use to cement focus and clarity, you'll also breathe in a greater peacefulness that will alter your larger relationship with your mind, your body, and your life. You will realize that the processes you have learned are repeatable, not just as approaches but as outcomes. And as a result, once you've conquered the *new* next thing, you'll be ready for the next thing after that—the next play, the next season, the next job, the next unknown.

NEXT WITH GRANT

Grant Parr, MA is available for coaching and consulting with elite athletes, coaches, and corporate executives through his consulting practice Gameface Performance, https://www.gamefaceperformance.com/.

His work extends to teams as well as to individuals, and he is also available for corporate or team speaking events, conferences, workshops, and keynote addresses.

ABOUT THE AUTHOR

Grant Parr, MA, is a mental sports performance coach focusing on high-impact and combat sports. His practice uses mental skills techniques and strategies to help athletes and coaches gain a competitive edge in their sports performances. He works with a wide variety of athletes and teams including Olympians, Olympic coaches, professional athletes, collegiate athletes, and high school athletes. His podcast, 90% Mental, provides a window into a broad range of athletes' and coaches' mental games and shares their insights around mental performance. Grant currently lives in San Francisco, California.

CPSIA information can be obtained
at www.ICGtesting.com
Printed in the USA
BVHW042302210419
546107BV00012B/238/P